Praise for *Cloud Computing and SOA Convergence in Your Enterprise*

"Cloud computing is a hot topic today in business circles for its potential to transform IT service delivery and galvanize service-oriented architecture. David Linthicum is one of the foremost authorities in the strategic application of technology to business, and this book is required reading for those looking to reap the rewards of cloud computing in the enterprise."

> Dion Hinchcliffe
> Enterprise Web 2.0 Expert and ZDNet blogger,
> President/CTO of Hinchcliffe & Company

"In this book, David Linthicum does that rarest of things: He manages to combine showing *why* SOA and cloud computing complement one another with a lucid game plan of *how* a business can take advantage of the synergies between them in concrete ways that will contribute to the bottom line."

> Jeremy Geelan
> Conference Chair, Cloud Computing Conference and Expo Series,
> Senior Vice President, SYS-CON Media & Events

"This book cuts through all of the hype and confusion of cloud computing and brings us back to the basics of architecture. Finally, someone wrote a book that is not just about semantics but instead guides us through a methodical approach for delivering solutions in the cloud. I highly recommend this book!"

> Mike Kavis
> Chief Technology Officer of MDot,
> Vice President and Director of Social Technologies for CAEAP

"David Linthicum has a talent for explaining how technology issues impact business decisions and strategy. Linthicum never gives you just another technical discussion about the latest tech fad. Instead, he explains the technology *and* the relevant business issues that both business and IT audiences need to understand before investing in cloud computing."

> Loraine Lawson
> Award-winning journalist and
> blogger for *IT Business Edge*

"As cloud computing stokes the embers of the SOA hype, practitioners can count on pragmatic and opportunistic advice from Dave Linthicum. Cloud computing brings time-to-value to SOA by leveraging other people's work. In this excellent guide book, Dave shares a step-by-step plan for organizations to determine which of their services, information, and processes are good candidates to reside in, and come from, the clouds."

> Brenda M. Michelson
> Principal, Elemental Links

Cloud Computing and SOA Convergence in Your Enterprise

Cloud Computing and SOA Convergence in Your Enterprise

A Step-by-Step Guide

David S. Linthicum

✦Addison-Wesley

Upper Saddle River, NJ • Boston • Indianapolis • San Francisco
New York • Toronto • Montreal • London • Munich • Paris • Madrid
Capetown • Sydney • Tokyo • Singapore • Mexico City

Many of the designations used by manufacturers and sellers to distinguish their products are claimed as trademarks. Where those designations appear in this book, and the publisher was aware of a trademark claim, the designations have been printed with initial capital letters or in all capitals.

The author and publisher have taken care in the preparation of this book, but make no expressed or implied warranty of any kind and assume no responsibility for errors or omissions. No liability is assumed for incidental or consequential damages in connection with or arising out of the use of the information or programs contained herein.

The publisher offers excellent discounts on this book when ordered in quantity for bulk purchases or special sales, which may include electronic versions and/or custom covers and content particular to your business, training goals, marketing focus, and branding interests. For more information, please contact:

U.S. Corporate and Government Sales
(800) 382-3419
corpsales@pearsontechgroup.com

For sales outside the United States, please contact:

International Sales
international@pearson.com

Visit us on the Web: informit.com/aw

Library of Congress Cataloging-in-Publication Data
Linthicum, David S., 1962–
    Cloud computing and SOA convergence in your enterprise : a step-by-step guide / David S. Linthicum.
        p.   cm.
    Includes bibliographical references and index.
    ISBN 0-13-600922-0 (pbk. : alk. paper)
    1. Web services. 2. Cloud computing. 3. Service-oriented architecture (Computer science) I. Title.
TK5105.88813L56 2009
006.7'8—dc22   2009027378

ISBN-13: 978-0-13-600922-1
ISBN   0-13-600922-0

Text printed in the United States on recycled paper at RR Donnelley Crawfordsville in Crawfordsville, Indiana.

2nd   Printing   June 2010

In memory of Spanky,
the world's greatest dog.
We all miss you.

Contents

Preface

The movement to cloud computing is the disruptive change that IT departments will soon face as service-oriented architecture (SOA) and cloud computing begin to have an effect on the modern enterprise. IT managers must learn how to give as well as take information in this new, shareable environment, while still protecting their company's interests. Innovative companies will take advantage of these new resources, such as cloud computing, and reinvent themselves as unstoppable forces in their markets. Those who do not take advantage of this revolution will become quickly outdated, perhaps going out of business. This book is your first step toward understanding the issues you will face as cloud computing and SOA converge, and toward opening the company gates to nurture this IT Renaissance while still keeping the barbarians at bay.

The movement and direction are clear. Take, for instance, the rapid rise of cloud computing. Based on current trends, Interactive Data Corporation (IDC) reports, "Over the next five years, IDC expects spending on IT cloud services to grow almost threefold, reaching $42 billion by 2012 and accounting for 9% of revenues in five key market segments. More importantly, spending on cloud computing will accelerate throughout the forecast period, capturing 25% of IT spending growth in 2012 and nearly a third of growth the following year."[1] This leaves IDC with no doubt that there is a fundamental shift toward cloud computing as a delivery mechanism and toward its use within the notion of SOA as an approach to marry cloud computing with the enterprise.

Moreover, a recent Gartner report shows global revenue from cloud computing will top $150 billion by 2013.[2] This projection includes revenue generated by the shift from on-premise to cloud-based providers as well as by the planning and architecture behind the shift.

What is causing this shift? There are five primary drivers:

1. Purchasers believe that the current cost of traditional enterprise software is disproportionate to the value it creates.
2. In these budget-conscious times, there is intense pressure to reduce the cost of acquisition and maintenance of software solutions (the ongoing support and maintenance of solutions can often be four times the original capital cost).
3. Organizations are striving to reduce risk, and they want a far more tangible relationship between software's benefit and cost.
4. The drive for reduced risk demands a much greater predictability of the running costs of the organization's software solutions.
5. The value of solutions is no longer determined by the functionality available (in fact, most organizations use only a small subset of the functions available in their software products) but by the feelings and experiences of the users in the way that they use and interact with the solution.

At the same time, enterprises are turning to SOAs to provide a platform for the use of cloud-delivered services and links to the emerging Web, even through the ad hoc notion of *mash-ups*. The movement toward SOA is well documented, like cloud computing, and is being driven faster by the emerging service-oriented resources within the clouds.

---

1. IDC Press Release. "IDC Finds Cloud Computing Entering Period of Accelerating Adoption and Poised to Capture IT Spending Growth over the Next Five Years." October 20, 2008. http://www.idc.com/getdoc.jsp?containerId=prUS21480708.
2. "Gartner: Cloud Computing Poised for Considerable Growth." Posted March 27, 2009. IT Business Edge Web site. http://www.itbusinessedge.com/cm/community/news/inf/blog/gartner-cloud-computing-poised-for-considerable-growth/?cs=31403.

According to Evans Data Corp.'s latest Web Services Development Survey, this year the percentage of functioning Service-Oriented Architectures (SOAs) has almost doubled. Web Services are also experiencing more comprehensive implementation with 30% of respondents using more than 20 services in the next year, a 58% increase from today.

—Evans Data Corp.

Moreover, there is a movement to leverage these pervasive services within the enterprise through mash-ups, providing on-demand access to business processes and information, as needed, and at bargain rates.

Mash-ups portend big changes for software companies, Web sites, and everyone online. No longer just a collection of pages, the Web is morphing into a sort of global operating system. . . . People are seizing far more control of what they do online. In the process, those efforts are putting skin on the bones of Web services, the long-delayed promise of software and services that can be tapped on demand.

—Business Week

What is important to remember is that a huge resource is being created on the Web among cloud computing providers. You must take advantage of this resource, otherwise it will devastate your enterprise in much the same way as when, in the early 1990s, those who ignored the rise of the Web soon found themselves playing catch-up. This is a similar megatrend, and the time is now to prepare your business to fit into this new cloud computing paradigm, which is actually much more complex than the traditional Web but provides 10 times the return on investment. This book shows you how the convergence of SOA and cloud computing will occur, what it is, and the steps you can take to align your IT with this revolutionary technology.

About the Book

This book is the bible for those looking to take advantage of the convergence of SOA and cloud computing. It includes detailed technical information about the trend, supporting technology and methods, a step-by-step guide for doing a self-evaluation, and an approach to reinventing your enterprise to become a connected, efficient, moneymaking machine. *Cloud Computing and SOA Convergence in Your Enterprise* is an idea-shifting book that will set the stage for the way IT is delivered for years to come. This is more than just a book that defines some technology; this book defines a class of technology as well as approaches and strategies to make things work within your enterprise.

As the author, I am the recognized authority in each of the disciplines that contribute to the convergence of SOA and cloud computing. My goal with this book is to properly communicate the notion of the convergence and lay down a course for this technology set and the change that needs to occur. I define things from the outside in, from the inside out, and at all points in between, building on groundbreaking concepts of the past, including EAI, B2B, Web Services, and SOA.

IT leaders, developers, and architects will find the information contained in *Cloud Computing and SOA Convergence in Your Enterprise* extremely useful. Many examples are used to make the information easier to understand, and ongoing support is available from the book's Web site. Prerequisites for this book are a basic understanding of Web Services, cloud computing, and related development tools and technologies at a high level. However, those of you who are not technical will find this book just as valuable as a means of understanding this revolution and how it will affect your enterprise.

Structure of the Book

My intent is to keep the chapters as short as possible and to the point. While I once defined my books by word count, this book is defined by NGIPC (number of good ideas per chapter). So, it is going to be a bit of a wild ride at times, but something you can read in a coast-to-coast plane ride. I use examples where I can and case studies when available. Moreover, I make sure to leverage outside resources where they make sense. You do not write a book like this within a vacuum of ideas.

Most of the information is delivered in the traditional chapter-to-chapter manner, but within these chapters are "Book Blogs" (sidebars) used to hammer home the points discussed in the regular text. I use the Book Blogs as quick brain dumps to enliven the topic.

This book is written for you, the poor person charged with doing a lot of IT with few resources. I want to make your work better. I want to make your company successful. This is different from other books I've written in the past, which were more about *what* something is. This book contains a bit of *what*, but more *how*, and that will make all the difference. You cannot do *what* if you do not know *how*.

Enjoy the ride.

　　　　　　　　　　　　　　　　　　　　　　　　　　　　　　　—Dave

Acknowledgments

There are a bunch of people to thank for this book, including Bernard Goodwin and Michelle Housley at Pearson, Inc. This book would not exist but for their faith in me, and I offer them my heartfelt thanks.

This book started its life with the working title *12 Steps to SOA*, which I proposed way back in 2005. Shortly after the proposal was accepted, I took a job as CEO of an overseas company. While I made my best efforts to get the book completed, the reality was that the book would surely be outdated by the time it hit the book stores. I had too many 80-hour work weeks and not enough time to focus on creating new concepts that would make that book truly valuable. Thus, I put the project aside after writing only a few chapters.

After four years of doing the entrepreneurial thing, including stints as a CTO once and a CEO twice, all with cloud computing companies, I decided to propose a new cloud computing-focused version of the book, and Bernard accepted it. This book would focus on extending SOA approaches to the world of cloud computing using a step-by-step approach with very clear guidance for those looking to leverage cloud computing in their enterprise. I felt this information was desperately needed in the market, and thus *Cloud Computing and SOA Convergence in Your Enterprise* was born. Or, I should say, reborn—in large part due to the patience of the wonderful folks at Pearson, who have been my publisher since 1997.

Of course, the book would not be as readable were it not for Linda Crippes, my copy editor and writing advisor, who has taken many paragraphs from near-gibberish to English. We have worked together for so long that, at this point, I am not sure when we started. I'm just glad to have somebody to assist in that department, since my brain works better in speaking mode than when I write.

I also want to thank the reviewers, including Mike, Joe, JP, and Ron, who provided some great feedback on this emerging topic. We are breaking new ground here, and it is always good to have a team of smart guys who make sure your ideas are not too crazy. I considered all of your comments and all of your suggestions and found them to be very, very useful.

Finally, I want to thank my wonderful clients who provided me with the experience required to write a book like this. I am in business to make them successful, and I feel privileged to say their successes reflect my own.

About the Author

David S. Linthicum (Dave) knows cloud computing and service-oriented architecture (SOA). He is an internationally recognized industry expert and thought leader and the author and coauthor of thirteen books on computing, including the best-selling *Enterprise Application Integration* (Addison-Wesley). Dave keynotes at many leading technology conferences on cloud computing, SOA, Web 2.0, and enterprise architecture, and he has appeared on a number of television and radio shows as a computing expert. He is a blogger for *InfoWorld, Intelligent Enterprise*, and eBizq.net, covering SOA and enterprise computing topics. Dave also has columns in *Government Computer News, Cloud Computing Journal, SOA Journal*, and *Align Journal*, and is the editor of *Virtualization Journal*.

In his career, Dave has formed or enhanced many of the ideas behind modern distributed computing, including enterprise application integration, B2B application integration, and SOA, all of which are approaches and technologies in wide use today. For the last ten years, Dave has focused on the technology and strategies around cloud computing and how to make cloud computing work for the modern enterprise. This includes work with several cloud computing startups.

Dave's industry experience includes tenure as CTO and CEO of several successful software companies and upper-level management positions in Fortune 100 companies. In addition, he was an associate professor of computer science for eight years and continues to lecture at major technical colleges and universities, including the University of Virginia, Arizona State University, and the University of Wisconsin.

CHAPTER 1

Where We Are, How We Got Here, and How to Fix It

There are painters who transform the sun to a yellow spot, but there are others who with the help of their art and their intelligence, transform a yellow spot into the sun.

—Pablo Picasso (1881–1973)

It is Thursday morning, you are the CEO of a large, publicly traded company, and you just called your executives into the conference room for the exciting news: the board of directors has approved the acquisition of a key competitor, and you are looking for a call-to-action to get everyone planning for the next steps.

You talk to the sales executives about the integration of both sales forces within three months, and they are excited about the new prospects. You talk to the human resources director, who is ready to address the changes HR must make within two months. You speak to the buildings and maintenance director, who can have everyone moved who needs to be moved within three months. Your heart is filled with pride.

However, when you ask the CIO about changing the core business processes to drive the combined companies, the response is much less enthusiastic. "I'm not sure we can change our IT architecture to accommodate the changes in less than 18 months, and I'm not even sure if that's possible," says the CIO. "We simply don't have the ability or the capacity to integrate these systems. We'll need new systems, a bigger data center. . . ." You get the idea.

As the CEO, you are nonplussed. While the other departments are able to accommodate the business opportunity in fewer than four months, IT needs almost two years?

In essence, IT has become the single-most visible point of latency when a business needs to change. Thus, the ability to change is limited by IT. In this case, the merger is not economically feasible, and the executive team is left scratching their heads. They thought IT was about new ways to automate the business and had no idea how slow the IT folks are to react to change.

However, it does not have to be this way. The survival of many businesses will depend on a fundamental change in the way we think about and create our IT infrastructure going forward—that is, if you are willing to admit where you are and are willing to change. There is much work to be done, and reading this book is a great first step.

How Things Got Off Track

IT issues are best understood by understanding its general history over the last 30 years as well as your company's specific IT history. History tells you why things are they way they are. Examining your company's IT history is almost like participating in a 12-step program: you admit you have a problem and are willing to look at how you got here.

It is also important that you check your ego at the door. IT folk typically do not like to talk about mistakes made in the past. Indeed, many will defend until the day they die all IT-related decisions that were made in the past. But the point of examining the IT history is not about placing blame—it is about recognizing what you are currently dealing with and discovering ways to fix it. If you cannot open your eyes and mind to the existing problems, then reading the rest of this book will do you very little good.

If there is one issue that comes to mind each and every time we look at IT's past mistakes, it is *managing-by-magazine*. In essence, those charged with building and managing IT systems often did not look at what was best for the business but looked instead at what was most popular at the time or at what was being promoted in the popular computer journals as the technology "required" to solve all problems.

Another issue is *managing-by-inertia*, or failing to do anything just because it is new and unknown. This problem is opposite to *managing-by-*

magazine: Instead of doing something just because it is popular, we simply sit on our existing IT architecture. Typically, this lack of action is rooted in the fear of change and the risks associated with it.

We had the structured computing revolution, which became the object-oriented computing revolution, which became distributed objects, which became component development, which became enterprise resource planning, which became customer relations management, which became service orientation—you get the idea. Of course, I am missing a bunch of other technologies that we "had to have," including data warehousing, business intelligence, business process management—the list goes on and on.

Not that these technologies were bad things; most were not. However, they had the effect of distracting those in IT from the core problems of their business and focusing their attention more on the productized technology than on the needs and requirements of the business. The distraction was easy because analyzing and documenting business requirements was not as fun as experimenting with new technologies and was not a résumé-enhancing experience.

This focus more on the solution than on the problem caused a layering effect within the enterprise architectures. In essence, the architectures grew more complex and cumbersome because the popular products of the day were being dragged into the data center and became another layer of complexity that both increased costs and made the enterprise architecture much too fragile, tightly coupled, and difficult to change.

Today we have IT infrastructures and enterprise architectures that are just too costly to maintain and difficult to impossible to change. As business needs change, including upturns and downturns in the economy, IT is having an increasingly harder time adjusting to meet the needs of business. As in our example at the beginning of this chapter, CEOs are finding that IT is typically the latency within the business that causes delays and cost overruns, and IT does not add value to the enterprise as it once did. Remember when IT was the solution and not the problem?

IT departments were more productive when they were coding applications in COBOL on mainframes because it required them to be lean and cautious with their use of resources. Today, we have almost too much technology and too many options. We gave IT enough rope to hang themselves, or at least to get their IT architectures in a state that makes them much less valuable to the business.

SOA to the Rescue?

While there are many attempts to fix the badly broken IT architectures within our enterprises, most "solutions" just put another technology layer on top of the existing technologies in hopes that the technology will somehow fix the issues. As you may have guessed, it just makes things more complex. Few enterprises were willing to take the risk and address the core issues.

Service-oriented architecture, or SOA, is really about fixing existing architectures by addressing most of the major systems as services and abstracting those services into a single domain where they are formed into solutions. Simple in concept—and really nothing new—SOA is our best approach to fixing the broken architectures. With the wide use of standards such as Web Services, SOA is being promoted as the best way to bring architectural agility to your enterprise—that is, if you do SOA correctly. There is no magic bullet here.

SOA is a valid approach to solve many of the architectural problems that enterprises face today. However, those who implement SOA typically look at SOA as something you buy, not something you do. Thus, many SOA projects are again about purchasing some technology that is sold as "SOA-in-a-box," which turns out to be in-a-box but not SOA, and thus only adds to the problems.

SOA, as the *A* implies, is architecture. And thus it is the orderly arrangement of systems that best serve the service needs of the business. Taken in its literal context, enterprise IT can succeed with SOA. However, most often it does not succeed, and much of that failure occurs because SOA implementers view SOA as something other than architecture, and most often those implementers are not architects.

SOA is a valid architectural pattern and one that is leveraged throughout this book, but you need to look at SOA as a journey, not a project, and clearly not a product. At the same time, you need to break SOA down into small, incremental successes that also move the enterprise toward the core value proposition of SOA, which becomes even more powerful when leveraged with emerging concepts such as cloud computing, the other focus of this book.

We can call this "small SOA" and "big SOA." Big SOA encompasses the larger strategic objectives of SOA: simultaneously moving all the enterprise IT assets to something much more agile and easy to change. An example would be breaking down all relevant enterprise systems to a functional primitive, building them up again as services, and adding a process configuration layer to form solutions. Considering that such an enterprise typically means hundreds and sometimes thousands of systems, this project could take many years.

Small SOA is just an instance of a big SOA. Small SOA is still SOA but has well-defined objectives, a time box, and a core return on investment that must be met. The lesson here is to leverage small SOA to get to big SOA. For instance, you could build a partner portal using SOA approaches that you can stand up in 6 months, with a return on investment of only three months— clear benefit and a small and doable project that occurs within a year's time.

While small SOA seems to be working, big SOA has largely been abandoned as too complex and too expensive to pursue. The reality is that you need both, but you need to know how to leverage both. Hold on to that thought for now. The topic of SOA is revisited many times in this book.

What the Heck Is SOA, and Why Should I Care?

First, let's put forth my definition of SOA so we have a foundation to work from.

> An SOA is a strategic framework of technology that allows all interested systems, inside and outside of an organization, to expose and access well-defined services, and information bound to those services, that may be further abstracted to process layers and composite applications for solution development. In essence, SOA adds the agility aspect to architecture, allowing us to deal with system changes using a configuration layer rather than constantly having to redevelop these systems.

The primary benefits of an SOA include

1. Reuse of services and behaviors, or the ability to leverage application behavior from application to application without a significant amount of recoding or integration. In other words, SOA enables use of the same application functionality (behavior) over and over again without having to port the code, leveraging remote application behavior as if it existed locally.
2. Agility, or the ability to change business processes on top of existing services and information flows, quickly and as needed, to support a changing business.

3. Monitoring, or the ability to monitor points of information and points of service, in real time, to determine the well-being of an enterprise or trading community. Moreover, SOA provides the ability to change and adjust processes for the benefit of the organization in real time.
4. Extended reach, or the ability to expose certain enterprise processes to other external entities for the purpose of interenterprise collaboration or shared processes. SOA can be used as a key technology-enabling approach to leverage cloud computing (described later in this chapter).

The notion of an SOA is not at all new. Attempts to share common processes, information, and services have a long history, one that began more than 10 years ago with multitier client/server—a set of shared services on a common server that provided the enterprise with the infrastructure for reuse and now provides for integration—and the distributed object movement. *Reusability* is a valuable objective. In the case of SOA, it is reuse of services and information bound to those services (see Figure 1.1). A common set of

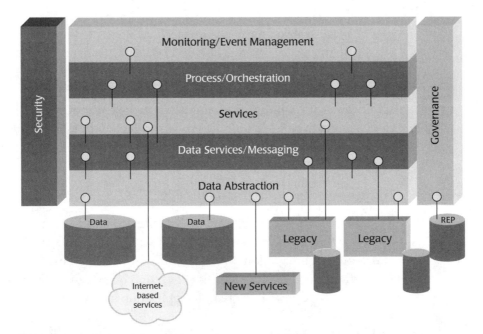

Figure 1.1 SOA metamodel provides a good way to see how SOA leverages a process/orchestration layer to change major business processes without driving changes to all systems. This is a loosely coupled architecture.

services among enterprise applications invites reusability and significantly reduces the need for redundant application services.

What is unique about SOA is that it is as much a strategy as a set of technologies, and it is really more of a journey than a destination.

SOA Meets Cloud Computing

So, what does SOA have to do with cloud computing, and why did we write a book about it? Cloud computing is any IT resource, including storage, database, application development, application services, and so on, that exists outside of the firewall that may be leveraged by enterprise IT over the Internet. The core idea behind cloud computing is that it is much cheaper to leverage these resources as services, paying as you go and as you need them, than it is to buy more hardware and software for the data center. There are other advantages as well.

Cloud computing allows you to expand and contract your costs in direct proportion to your needs. Moreover, it shifts some of the risk around expanding your IT resources from the enterprise to the cloud computing provider. We cover the business benefits of cloud computing in Chapter 4, "Making the Business Case for Clouds." Also, cloud computing abstracts those using the cloud computing–delivered IT resource from the management of those resources.

The relationship between cloud computing and SOA is that cloud computing provides IT resources you can leverage on demand, including resources that host data, services, and processes. Thus, you have the ability to extend your SOA outside of the enterprise firewall to cloud computing providers, seeking the benefits already described. We describe this process as "SOA using cloud computing," and it is the objective of this book to show you how it is done.

SOA is important to cloud computing for a few key reasons:

- It is a good approach to architecture that deals with the proper formation of the information systems using mechanisms that make them work and play well together, inside and outside of the enterprise.
- In order to take advantage of cloud computing, you need interfaces and architectures that can reach out and touch cloud computing resources. While many believe they can simply create quick and dirty links between core enterprise information systems and cloud computing resources, the

fact is that you really need an architecture inside of the enterprise, such as SOA, to make the most of cloud computing. That is the theme of this book.

■ You need some sort of architectural discipline with guiding principles to document and organize your architecture. Most have ignored this need over the past several years to focus on ad hoc hype-drive stuff. We must get back to leveraging the best solution for the problem, and SOA is a good approach for doing that if you follow the steps.

For our purposes, we know that cloud computing is the ability to provide IT resources over the Internet. These resources are typically provided on a subscription basis that can be expanded or contracted as needed. This includes storage services, database services, information services, testing services, security services, platform services—pretty much anything you can find in the data center today can be found on the Internet and delivered as a service.

If you think you have seen this movie before, you are right. Cloud computing is based on the time-sharing model we leveraged years ago before we could afford our own computers. The idea is to share computing power among many companies and people, thereby reducing the cost of that computing power to those who leverage it. It was a pretty simple idea at the time. The value of time share and the core value of cloud computing are pretty much the same, only the resources these days are much better and more cost effective. Moreover, you can mix and match them to form solutions, which was not possible with the traditional time-sharing model.

There is nothing to fear from cloud computing. Indeed, it should be comforting to leverage resources that you do not have to maintain. Moreover, the sharing model has been around for years—we just call it something new: cloud computing. There are also some new offerings in this space that we discuss next.

The opportunity to learn how to leverage cloud computing—in the context of well-known architectural approaches such as SOA—is a way to get your enterprises leveraging a more efficient and effective IT infrastructure. However, cloud computing is not a cure-all or something that you attach to your systems and hope for the best. You have to do some planning to leverage cloud computing resources in the right way. In essence, that is what this book is about.

Defining Cloud Computing

While cloud computing is widely defined, we need a standard definition for the purposes of this book. The National Institute of Standards and Technology (NIST), Information Technology Laboratory, provides the most comprehensive definition of cloud computing thus far offered.

Cloud computing is a pay-per-use model for enabling available, convenient, on-demand network access to a shared pool of configurable computing resources (e.g., networks, servers, storage, applications, services) that can be rapidly provisioned and released with minimal management effort or service provider interaction. This cloud model promotes availability and comprises five *key characteristics:*

- *On-demand self-service.* A consumer can unilaterally provision computing capabilities, such as server time and network storage, as needed without requiring human interaction with each service's provider.
- *Ubiquitous network access.* Capabilities are available over the network and accessed through standard mechanisms that promote use by heterogeneous thin or thick client platforms (e.g., mobile phones, laptops, and PDAs).
- *Location-independent resource pooling.* The provider's computing resources are pooled to serve all consumers using a multitenant model, with different physical and virtual resources dynamically assigned and reassigned according to consumer demand. The customer generally has no control over or knowledge of the exact location of the provided resources. Examples of resources include storage, processing, memory, network bandwidth, and virtual machines.
- *Rapid elasticity.* Capabilities can be rapidly and elastically provisioned to quickly scale up, and rapidly released to quickly scale down. To the consumer, the capabilities available for rent often appear to be infinite and can be purchased in any quantity at any time.
- *Pay per use.* Capabilities are charged using a metered, fee-for-service, or advertising-based billing model to promote optimization of resource use. Examples are measuring the storage, bandwidth, and computing resources consumed and charging for the number of active user accounts per month. Clouds within an organization accrue cost among business units and may or may not use actual currency.

Note that cloud software takes full advantage of the cloud paradigm by being service oriented with a focus on statelessness, low coupling, modularity, and semantic interoperability.[1] However, all cloud computing approaches are not the same, and several deployment models, while different, are still considered cloud computing:

- *Private cloud.* The cloud infrastructure is owned or leased by a single organization and is operated solely for that organization.
- *Community cloud.* The cloud infrastructure is shared by several organizations and supports a specific community that has shared concerns (e.g., mission, security requirements, policy, and compliance considerations).
- *Public cloud.* The cloud infrastructure is owned by an organization selling cloud services to the general public or to a large industry group.
- *Hybrid cloud.* The cloud infrastructure is a composition of two or more clouds (internal, community, or public) that remain unique entities but are bound together by standardized or proprietary technology that enables data and application portability (e.g., cloud bursting).

Each deployment model instance has one of two types: internal or external. Internal clouds reside within an organization's network security perimeter, and external clouds reside outside the same perimeter. For the purposes of this book, we focus primarily on public cloud computing, or the use of a public cloud provider or providers to host portions of our SOA. Many businesses will find that private clouds are a better solution for their situation, leveraging the benefits of cloud computing but within their firewall. Or, they may choose to leverage a mixture of public and private clouds, or a hybrid cloud. Finally, some may create semiprivate or community clouds, which are public clouds leveraged only by a closed group of companies or government agencies.

The message is that it is all cloud computing and all of these architectural options are available to you. The steps highlighted in this book are applicable to private, community, and hybrid cloud computing[2] as well as to public cloud computing. We cover private clouds in a bit more detail in Chapter 12, "Moving Onward."

---

1. http://csrc.nist.gov/groups/SNS/cloud-computing/index.html
2. Ibid.

The Components of Cloud Computing

As cloud computing emerges, there is a lot of discussion about how to describe it as a computing model. Maturity models have been published and debated, and providers clearly have a model for their own products.

In attempting to better describe cloud computing, we came up with a "stack" of sorts, which logically considers each component of cloud computing and how the components interact. While clearly this model could be much more complex, it does not need to be. This stack explanation is a model for defining and refining the concept of cloud computing (see Figure 1.2).

While many in the industry can debate the components, there are 11 major categories or patterns of cloud computing technology:

1. Storage-as-a-service
2. Database-as-a-service
3. Information-as-a-service
4. Process-as-a-service
5. Application-as-a-service
6. Platform-as-a-service
7. Integration-as-a-service

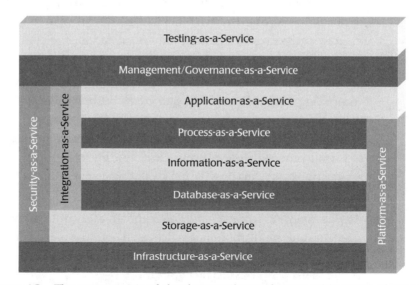

Figure 1.2   The components of cloud computing make up a wide range of services you can leverage over the Web through a subscription arrangement. Most services that you can leverage from a data center can now be leveraged from the cloud.

8. Security-as-a-service
9. Management/governance-as-a-service
10. Testing-as-a-service
11. Infrastructure-as-a-service

We go into more detail in Chapter 3, "Defining Clouds for the Enterprise," but it is useful to define them at a high level here.

Storage-as-a-service (also known as disk space on demand), as you may expect, is the ability to leverage storage that physically exists at a remote site but is logically a local storage resource to any application that requires storage. This is the most primitive component of cloud computing and is a component or pattern that is leveraged by most of the other cloud computing components.

Database-as-a-service (DaaS) provides the ability to leverage the services of a remotely hosted database, sharing it with other users and having it logically function as if the database were local. Different models are offered by different providers, but the power is to leverage database technology that would typically cost thousands of dollars in hardware and software licenses.

Information-as-a-service is the ability to consume any type of information, remotely hosted, through a well-defined interface such as an API. Examples include stock price information, address validation, and credit reporting.

Process-as-a-service is remote resource that can bind many resources together, such as services and data, either hosted within the same cloud computing resource or remotely, to create business processes. You can think of a business process as a meta-application that spans systems, leveraging key services and information that are combined into a sequence to form a process. These processes are typically easier to change than are applications and thus provide agility to those who leverage these process engines that are delivered on demand.

Application-as-a-service (AaaS), also known as software-as-a-service (SaaS), is any application that is delivered over the platform of the Web to an end user, typically leveraging the application through a browser. While many people associate application-as-a-service with enterprise applications such as Salesforce SFA, office automation applications are indeed applications-as-a-service as well, including Google Docs, Gmail, and Google Calendar.

Platform-as-a-service (PaaS) is a complete platform, including application development, interface development, database development, storage, testing, and so on, delivered through a remotely hosted platform to subscribers. Based on the traditional time-sharing model, modern platform-as-a-service providers provide the ability to create enterprise-class applications for use locally or on demand for a small subscription price or for free.

Integration-as-a-service is the ability to deliver a complete integration stack from the cloud, including interfacing with applications, semantic mediation, flow control, integration design, and so on. In essence, integration-as-a-service includes most of the features and functions found within traditional enterprise application integration (EAI) technology but delivered as a service.

Security-as-a-service, as you may have guessed, is the ability to deliver core security services remotely over the Internet. While the typical security services provided are rudimentary, more sophisticated services such as identity management are becoming available.

Management/governance-as-a-service (MaaS and GaaS) is any on-demand service that provides the ability to manage one or more cloud services. These are typically simple things such topology, resource utilization, virtualization, and uptime management. Governance systems are becoming available as well, offering, for instance, the ability to enforce defined policies on data and services.

Testing-as-a-service (TaaS) is the ability to test local or cloud-delivered systems using testing software and services that are remotely hosted. It should be noted that while a cloud service requires testing unto itself, testing-as-a-service systems have the ability to test other cloud applications, Web sites, and internal enterprise systems, and they do not require a hardware or software footprint within the enterprise.

Infrastructure-as-a-service (IaaS) is actually data center-as-a-service, or the ability to remotely access computing resources. In essence, you lease a physical server that is yours to do with as you will and, for all practical purposes, is your data center, or at least part of a data center. The difference with this approach versus more mainstream cloud computing is that instead of using an interface and a metered service, you have access to the entire machine and the software on that machine. In short, it is less packaged.

The Dream Team of Cloud Computing and SOA

While you can certainly leverage a cloud without practicing SOA, and you can leverage SOA without leveraging cloud computing, the real value of cloud computing is the ability to use services, data, and processes that can exist outside of the firewall in SEDC (somebody else's datacenter). Those who attempt to toss things to the clouds without some architectural forethought will find that cloud computing does not provide the value. Indeed, it could knock you back a few steps when considering the risks and cost of migration.

There will be some core patterns of success with cloud computing over the forthcoming years. Those who leverage cloud computing within the context of an architecture will succeed, while those who just toss things into the clouds as they think they need to will fail. Remember, SOA can provide a compelling business proposition when combined with cloud computing and an enterprise that needs this type of solution (see Figure 1.3).

Indeed, one can consider cloud computing the extension of SOA out to cloud-delivered resources, such as storage-as-a-service, data-as-a-service, platform-as-a-service—you get the idea (see Figure 1.4). The trick is to determine which services, information, and processes are good candidates to reside in the clouds as well as which cloud services should be abstracted within the existing or emerging SOA. We take you through that process in Chapters 4 through 11.

Simply put, you can think of clouds as additional places to run things. The advantage is that you do not have to drag yet another software-rich server into the data center along with the people required to maintain it.

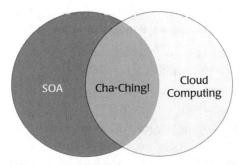

Figure 1.3 SOA and cloud computing provide a great deal of value when they work together.

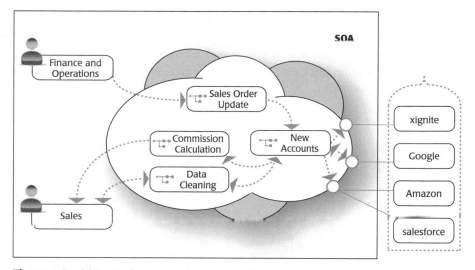

Figure 1.4 SOA can leverage cloud computing resources as services and use them as if they were contained within the SOA.

While enterprise IT is understandably skittish about cloud computing, many of the cloud computing resources out there will actually provide better service than on-premise utilities, once we allow cloud computing to settle in a bit more. Cloud computing benefits will continue to cushion the settling-in process, including cost savings, efficiencies, and access to thousands of dynamic Web-delivered resources.

Interest in cloud computing is also driving an interest in SOA. SOA not only is a mechanism to drive more reuse and agility but also offers the ability to figure out what should stay local and what should find a place in the clouds. Good SOA leads to a good cloud computing strategy, which leads to reduced costs, enhanced agility, and more excitement around enterprise computing than we have seen in awhile.

What SOA Can Learn from Cloud Computing

Service Design

Those who deploy services in the cloud, such as Amazon, Force.com, and others, have done a pretty good job with service design. You really *must* do a good job to rent the darn things out. Many SOA projects have a tendency to build in services that are too course-grained, too fine-grained, or just not at all well designed. We discuss this issue in more detail later in the book when we talk about service design and modeling for our SOA using cloud computing.

In reality, unless services are not well defined and well designed, they will not sell well when delivered on demand. Those who provide services out of the cloud—which are most major cloud computing providers—therefore must spend a lot of time on the design of the services, including usability and durability. We urge those who build services within their SOA, no matter the enabling technology and standards involved, to look at the existing services available for rent as good examples of how services should be designed, developed, and deployed.

Service Expandability

Cloud computing services are designed to expand as needed, and those who leverage cloud services do so because they can get the services on demand, when they need them. The ability to expand services within an SOA is typically a painful and expensive process.

The fact is that services designed and developed within enterprises typically are not designed to scale. Indeed, the core issues with SOA revolve around the fact that many within IT do not focus on scaling until it is too late and too difficult to fix. Cloud computing providers had to figure out scaling rather quickly.

What Cloud Computing Can Learn from SOA

Service Governance

There is little notion of governance today within cloud computing, and thus there is little control and implementation of policies. Therefore, many enterprises are not diving right into cloud computing.

Governance, while not always well implemented, is a fundamental fact of life with SOA. The ability to set policies around services and to manage changes to those services is a critical success factor. As we weave cloud computing–delivered services into applications and within our SOA, we will find that many things break as the on-demand services change over time. Typically, SOA can manage the changes through SOA governance systems, but perhaps some of that governance should originate with the services that come out of the clouds.

Driving from the Architecture

Doing SOA properly means driving SOA from the architecture to the technology. Within the world of cloud computing, the resources on demand are the starting point. With cloud computing, the need for a well-thought-out architecture is just as important as for traditional systems, considering that you are extending the architecture out of the firewall.

Using cloud computing resources is about extending your architecture out of the enterprise to incorporate cloud resources, and thus it is important to remember that your architecture does not end at the firewall. Understanding both the resources that exist within the enterprise and the resources that are cloud-delivered is even more critical, as is the need to configure these resources correctly in the context of an architecture and to meet the needs of the business.

Clearly, SOA and cloud computing go hand in hand. Cloud computing is just the ability to leverage new platforms and resources that you do not happen to own. Nothing really changes outside of that, including the need to do SOA right. However, cloud computing is accelerating the adoption of SOA by providing aspects of SOA on demand. SOA can learn a lot from the clouds, and the clouds can learn a lot from SOA. This book brings the two together.

Making the Leap

If you purchased this book, clearly we do not have to sell you much on making the leap to the clouds. The trick is to make sure you leap in the right direction. There are a few things to remember before you embark on the journey of extending your enterprise architecture to the cloud and to keep in mind as you read this book.

First, the switch to cloud computing is not about a quick fix; it is about moving your IT architecture incrementally forward, leveraging approaches around SOA and cloud computing resources when they make sense. Those who want to drive to changes in IT quickly and tactically will find useful information here, but a bit of architectural planning is strongly recommended. So, get excited, but stay on topic.

Second, look at the people and process issues within your enterprise at the same time you look at the technology. Many technologists miss this part and end up doing a very good job of driving toward a new architecture, but if nobody accepts it or pays for it, it is all for naught. Those who are successful with any systemic architecture change take into consideration the people and cultural issues.

Third, make sure to define the business case. We believe so strongly in defining the business case that we devote Chapter 4 to this topic. IT professionals need to get in the habit of working from the business to the architecture and then to the technology. All changes to the existing information systems should be justified as a clear business case, and the IT team should have to sell this change to the stakeholders and sponsors within the organization. If the change does not ultimately bring value to the bottom line, it should not be done.

Finally, do not get caught up in the hype—at least not too caught up. It is not productive when conversations around SOA and cloud computing degrade into debates around technology or standards before the problem is even clearly understood. We love to do that because we love technology.

Being Positively Disruptive

The idea is to drive change for the better. Many enterprises are in such bad shape that it makes sense to leverage disruptive technology and approaches to drive that change. This is really about rethinking, redefining, and shaking things up. The use of SOA using cloud computing is analogous to the first movement to the Web years ago. The use of the Web revolutionized the way we access and view information, and cloud computing will revolutionize the way we look at IT resources. It is about making major disruptive changes to very poorly planned IT infrastructures that drive changes for the good.

You must keep in mind as you read this book that the shift to cloud computing is all about change for the better using intense approaches and technologies that make sense. It is also about changing hearts and minds about adapting these technologies and approaches, and in essence, that is the most difficult part of the journey.

Many of you will face resistance from people in your organization who are reluctant to support the change. While many who drive disruptive change tend to view their reluctance as a hindrance, it is really an opportunity for you to test your ideas and learn how to explain them. Testing your ideas means listening to the points made by those resisting the change and using those points to see if you have missed anything in your assessment of what must be changed and why. While the naysayers may be overly negative at times, you need to welcome the opportunity to review your approaches and perhaps make revisions based on their feedback. You will have a firmer belief that what you are doing is right and perhaps will gain new knowledge and insights in the process.

Your role as teacher gives you the opportunity to learn how to educate people about what you are doing, and why. Those who are most successful in driving positive disruptive change are those who can thoroughly and with conviction explain the value of the new approach and new technologies.

The benefit for you is that if you successfully shift your company to a cloud computing and SOA architecture, your enterprises will be much more effective and efficient, able to meet most, if not all, of the needs of the business. You will have a key competitive advantage that allows you to increase your market share, build better products, and live up to the mission of the organization. You will have a healthy IT infrastructure that enables you to do more with less.

CHAPTER 2

Reaching for the Clouds

*They always say time changes things, but you
actually have to change them yourself.*
—Andy Warhol (1928–1987)

In Chapter 1, we talked about issues with existing enterprise architectures, but from this point on, we do not talk about how bad things are. Doing so is unproductive until we tell you how to solve these problems using disruptive approaches and technology, especially cloud computing, and explain how cloud computing works and plays well with service-oriented architecture (SOA).

This chapter is the jumping-off point for the subsequent chapters that dive more deeply into the core topics, things that you need to understand to address the core needs of your architecture, including how to fix problems by using best practices, SOA, and cloud computing.

There are a few other issues to consider here:

- Cloud computing is not the savior of IT. It is nothing but a way to deploy your enterprise architecture in a way that has the potential to be more productive and cost effective. In essence, it is a tool, not a way of life. It is not magic, it is not even new, but if approached correctly, it could be a path toward efficiency.
- Cloud computing and SOA are different concepts, but they are related. SOA is a pattern of architecture,

whereas cloud computing is an instance of architecture, or an architectural option. SOA is more holistic and strategic, meaning it deals with the complete enterprise including the business drivers, whereas cloud computing is more tactical and is a way of solving a problem. They are linked, and it is difficult to do one without the other if you are looking to solve problems at the enterprise level.

▪ The concepts of cloud computing require that many enterprises perform unnatural acts, such as outplacing processes and information. There are things to consider, of course, but there should never be an approach that is completely against cloud computing or completely for it. The answer is somewhere in the middle.

This book is not advocating cloud computing. Keep that in mind. It is a book promoting good architectural practices by leveraging the best from SOA and cloud computing. You get the balanced view here, including when cloud computing is a fit and when it is not. Cloud computing is not "the end of IT," nor is it a waste of time. Its value is somewhere between the two extremes.

You will never hear from me that you need to outplace your core information systems to cloud-based platforms—nor will you hear that you do not need to look into it. It is a balancing act that requires you to understand your own issues before you can implement any approaches or techniques to build a better IT infrastructure for your enterprise.

Diving Deeper into Cloud Computing

Now, what the heck is cloud computing? It seems simple, but many define it in very different ways. From our discussion in Chapter 1, we defined cloud computing as follows:

Cloud computing is the ability to provide IT resources over the Internet. These resources are typically provided on a subscription basis that can be expanded or contracted as needed. Services include storage services, database services, information services, testing services, security services, platform services—pretty much anything you can find in the data center today can be found on the Internet and delivered as a service.

In many respects, cloud computing is about abstracting the cloud computing resource from the underlying hardware and software, which are remotely hosted. Thus, you deal with the service and almost never with the needs and requirements of the platform, including maintenance, monitoring, and the cost of the hardware and data center space. More simply put, cloud computing is

- Stuff you do not own.
- Stuff you do not maintain, at least from an infrastructure point of view.
- Stuff you do not see.
- Stuff you pay for as a subscription or perhaps get for free.
- Expandable on demand.
- Reducible on demand.

The concept is to leverage computing resources that you do not own or maintain, and thereby lower the cost of computing through economies of scale. The more that organizations share cloud computing resources, the less they should cost (see Figure 2.1).

Moreover, you can leverage computing resources that provide more prebuilt component parts and thereby avoid having to build everything from

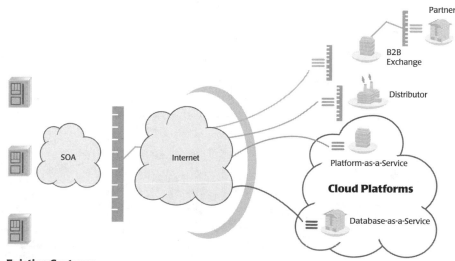

Existing Systems

Figure 2.1 Cloud computing provides access to shared resources.

scratch. You can find many bits and pieces of an application within the clouds and get much farther down the road than if you built your system from scratch.

A good example of a use case is a data service to provide credit check information. You can host the data yourself and build the interface using traditional technology. Or, you can leverage one of dozens of service providers in the cloud to provide the required information through a Web API (see Figure 2.2), which is typically a Web Service (information-as-a-service). You would leverage this service as if it were local to the applications that use it, despite that it could be thousands of miles away. All of this, if done correctly, is transparent to those who use the application.

The difference is in operating costs and speed to market. In the build-it-and-host-it-yourself scenario, in some circumstances, the cost is a few times more than if you find that same functionality and information in the cloud. Moreover, it typically takes more time to get the darn thing up and running if you build it yourself. Considering maintenance costs, human resources needed, and the fact that the service you are leveraging is not your company's core business, the case for the cloud becomes even more compelling. The fit for cloud computing, however, is going to be based on the needs of the par-

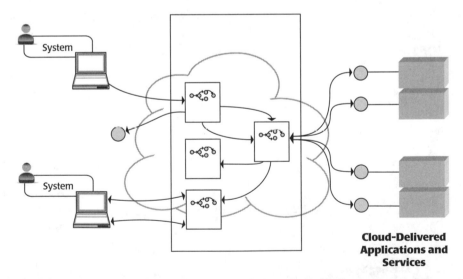

Cloud-Delivered Applications and Services

Figure 2.2 Cloud computing allows you to leverage application components you do not have to build.

ticular enterprise. As we see in Chapter 4, "Making the Business Case for Clouds," you have to do the business case for cloud computing, for each problem domain, in order to determine the real value that it will bring.

Clearly, not all systems should exist in the cloud. When considered holistically with the purpose of the system and the core requirements, the system could actually cost more when placed in clouds. Thus, you must apply some critical thinking around the use of cloud computing and SOA. Make sure to define cloud computing as part of the architecture, and make all of the business cases for it, considering all of the variables, including hard and soft costs. Again, we touch more on the business case for cloud computing in Chapter 4.

Now that you understand the value, how do you figure out what needs to be in the cloud and what needs to be local to the enterprise? As with all things related to enterprise computing, it depends on your enterprise. However, there are steps you can take to figure out your requirements. We discuss those steps in later chapters.

What's New in the Clouds?

The common question coming from those who are just beginning to look at cloud computing and the value it can bring to the enterprise seems to be *What's new in the clouds?* Those who are deep into cloud computing already—typically vendors and consultants—are actually having trouble answering that question, and for good reason: the concepts behind cloud computing have been in use for decades.

Cloud computing can be thought of as "time-sharing," or the ability to share computing resources among many different users. In the early days of computing, many companies actually shared a single computer that was located in a remote data center. The computer was able to allocate and manage resources for each user and each application, and users could request more computing time, or less, adjusting the amount of time they used the time-sharing service.

So, what does modern cloud computing offer that is new to enterprise IT?

First is the ability to leverage components from different cloud resources and mix and match the solutions you are seeking. You can leverage storage-as-a-service from one provider, database-as-a-service from another, and even a complete application development and deployment platform from a third. This ability to leverage just the resources you need from the solutions you want to drive, as well as in just the right amounts, is a clear value of modern cloud computing.

Second is the commoditization of bandwidth, which allows enterprises to leverage cloud computing resources as if they are local. Thus, you can leverage storage and runtime resources as if they existed within your data center, something that was difficult just a few years ago.

Finally, there is the availability of very innovative cloud computing providers. While the architecture and model of cloud computing is nothing new, the cloud computing players who provide the services are, including infrastructure-as-a-service players such as Amazon's EC2 and platform-as-a-service players such as Google's App Engine. With cloud computing growing by leaps and bounds, better and more innovative cloud computing services are being built and released continuously.

There are clear differences between early time sharing and modern cloud computing, but those who have been around for awhile see some very familiar patterns. As we move forward with cloud computing, the idea is to leverage cloud computing as another tool in the shed that has the potential to make your enterprise architecture more cost effective and efficient.

However, as with any new technology trend, cloud computing is not a silver bullet that you can shoot at every conceivable IT problem and expect good results. There is nothing here we have not dealt with before, so it should not be that scary, and we should understand the value of cloud computing and other architectural options.

Where SOA Meets the Clouds

If you want to provide real value to your enterprise, SOA should extend out of the firewall and onto cloud computing platforms. However, this is not universally accepted by the rank-and-file SOA guys. Generally speaking, most view SOA as something that occurred exclusively within the firewall. Extending the reach of their SOA to Internet-based resources was taboo. Indeed, within most enterprises, Web-delivered resources, such as cloud services, are not in use. In most cases, fear, more than any real issues they may have, prevents companies from adopting this new technology approach. We discuss resistance to cloud computing and SOA in much more detail in Chapter 12, "Moving Onward."

Cloud computing is really SOA that uses Internet-based resources, including services, applications, directories, tools, and so on, and generally accepts that it is okay to place business processes outside of the firewall (see Figure 2.3). It is not a replacement for SOA or traditional enterprise architecture, but it is an approach to architecture in which there is a core acceptance that Internet-based resources may provide the fastest delivery, the largest number of resources, and a minimum cost.

The general notion is that cloud computing provides another location for core business processes using outsourced infrastructure and reusable business processes that are accessible on demand. These Internet-borne systems and architectures in many cases provide better development speed, access to prebuilt resources, and much more value when compared to traditional enterprise approaches. These are the reasons SOA proves itself on the platform of the Web more so than within the enterprise these days: It is faster and easier, and it provides more initial return on investment.

The adoption of "Internet-borne SOA," or the notion of extending your SOA to cloud providers, is finding quick acceptance. Most SOA patterns exist outside of enterprises on the platform of the Web while architects still struggle with SOA within the enterprise.

Composite applications are being built with emerging on-demand tools. Those applications will need information, services, and APIs, also delivered on demand over the Internet. Enterprises will seek to externalize existing enterprise data to the cloud as well, and thus user management and security will remain core issues. In just a few years, we could see many enterprises with more business processes running outside of the firewall than within—if we can get enterprise architects to read this book.

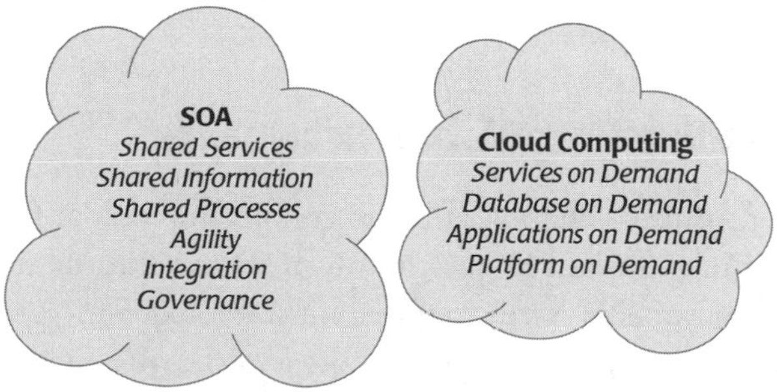

SOA
Shared Services
Shared Information
Shared Processes
Agility
Integration
Governance

Cloud Computing
Services on Demand
Database on Demand
Applications on Demand
Platform on Demand

Figure 2.3 Where the cloud meets SOA.

The Potential Value of the Clouds

What will cloud computing bring to your bottom line? In essence, this is the process of calculating the return on investment for the formation of clouds around your enterprise. However, keep in mind that not all systems make sense to outsource, and you have to be honest about the real costs and benefits. We take a much deeper dive into the business case in Chapter 4, but we address a few basic concepts here.

The first step is to determine the "as-is" state of a particular application and/or business system, including the cost of operations, maintenance, design, development, testing, deployment, and so on. From there, you determine the "to-be" state with cloud computing resources.

In addition, you need to define the value of agility and expandability, or the ability to change the information systems quickly as business needs change, and the ability to scale or expand the systems as the processing load needs to increase to support the business.

Finally, you need to consider the ability for your applications to take advantage of other services, information, and applications that exist on cloud computing platforms, avoiding having to write them from scratch. Make sure to document all of this information and come up with a return on investment that the business can expect—or not expect. You determine the need to proceed at this point.

While most IT professionals think the value of cloud computing is widely understood, the reality is that cloud computing requires some complex analysis to determine its value. Indeed, many dimensions must be considered, including the real cost of porting, the form and fit for the application, security issues, compliance issues, and the cost of trusting another organization you do not control. Again, we cover these issues in more detail in Chapter 4.

Cloud Computing Benefits and Drawbacks

Most of those who look at cloud computing look at the single dimension of cost. While you can look at an on-premise solution and a cloud computing solution as just a hardware and software acquisition lease-versus-buy decision, the reality is that the benefits and drawbacks to cloud computing are much more complex and far reaching.

As the hype progresses, you will only hear about the benefits. However, those who consider cloud computing as a way to improve their enterprise architecture must understand the benefits of the medicine as well as the side effects. That is the only way to figure out if you want or need the treatment.

Benefits

1. Cost
2. Network
3. Innovative
4. Expandability
5. Speed to implementation
6. It's green

Cost means that cloud computing, as an architectural solution, is typically less expensive than solutions deployed in traditional data centers when considering the cost of the hardware, software, and human resources that have to maintain the systems. While cloud computing is not always less expensive, it is, at least conceptually, more cost effective.

Host or Cloud?

To develop a new system, you must pay for development and you must design for peak loads, which results in excess capacity that often goes unused. The need to build in this excess capacity means that your investment in hardware and software will be underutilized most of the time.

Cloud services should be less expensive because you pay only for what you use. If you are working with an existing system—that is, trying to decide whether to wrap a legacy system as a service or to a cloud service—the case is less compelling, because many of the in-house expenditures have already been made and amortized.

You have to consider all of these points in your cloud-versus-host decision.

Since cloud providers use a pay-as-you-go or an on-demand model, there is a reasonable usage fee, typically based on time, units of storage, or other means of monetizing their clouds. Cost is the core benefit of cloud computing, since you pay just for what you use.

Moreover, there is more cost savings when you consider that you are done with beta and version .0 releases. Since clouds are as-a-service and remotely hosted, the cloud provider can update, fix, or redeploy software anytime, as needed, and typically without bothering the cloud user. Those who have suffered through software upgrades will find this a huge advantage. However, the lack of control over when fixes and updates are performed can be costly to the cloud user. If not performed when needed, fixes—actually, the lack thereof—can cripple the cloud user. Updates can force the cloud user into costly, untimely, and possibly unwanted changes, especially as older versions are retired.

Network means the clouds are in the Internet, and the Internet is connected to many other things that add value, including social networking sites, commerce APIs, mapping APIs, and other clouds. Thus, you can better mix and match cloud services to meet the needs of the business problem you are looking to solve. The ability for a cloud service to be combined with other cloud services, making a custom service that is even more powerful than the sum of any of its parts, is a real benefit of cloud computing.

Innovative means that cloud computing and the solutions it provides now are new, modern, and innovative, and it will continue to have a lot of innovative features that provide a lot of value for the money invested. This makes cloud computing a much easier sell, since the hype, the passion, and the majority of those in the industry are behind cloud computing because it is known to provide value. That in itself has value. Those companies that leverage cloud computing, particularly startups, will find that the use of this approach adds to the value of the IT innovations they created and thus to the company as a whole.

Expandability, somewhat related to cost, means that you can add as much capacity as you need, when you need it, just by increasing spending. Also, you can reduce the capacity just as easily. There is no need to place a ton of hardware and software in the wings just waiting for an opportunity to go into production. Nor will you get caught needing resources that take weeks or months to acquire and install. You can get what you need, when you need it, and with the click of a mouse.

Speed to implementation, also related to expandability, is a benefit because the time to implementation of cloud computing can be days, perhaps just hours in some cases. You are not purchasing hardware, installing operating systems, or getting permission to take a portion of a data center. You simply sign up, in most cases, and then you have access to the cloud resources in need. Those who have gone through hardware and software buys, installation, testing, deployment, and the fun of dealing with the people you need to deal with to get your stuff up and running will recognize the benefit of this aspect of cloud computing.

It's green means that cloud computing is good for the environment. If you are worried about the environment, you will be happy to know that cloud computing is the greenest approach to computing out there. The ability to share computing resources, and thus to shut down very power-hungry data centers, reduces the need for electric power.

While its "greenness" allows you to argue when selling cloud computing that those against it also hate polar bears, chances are that being green is more of an afterthought than a major value proposition. However, while many huge corporations are calling themselves green these days, cloud computing will provide them a chance to walk the walk. Most green corporations still maintain humongous data centers and thousands of services, mainframes, storage devices, and other things that have huge carbon footprints. That's not very green.

Drawbacks

1. Security
2. Control
3. Cost
4. Openness
5. Compliance
6. Service-level agreements

Security means that cloud computing–delivered infrastructure, because it is not under your direct control, has the potential to leave your information exposed in some cases. While cloud computing providers support encryption, user name and password–level security, and even rudimentary identity management, you still do not want to place state secrets in the clouds these days. However, most business information does not include state secrets and is perfectly fine for cloud computing. Moreover, cloud computing is getting better at security as time goes on, and there is no reason to expect that information residing on cloud computing platforms is not as secure as, or even more secure than, on-premise systems. This is just another issue to consider.

Control means that when you leverage a cloud computing provider, you are giving up control of that aspect of your IT infrastructure. While doing so is perhaps an emotional thing for the "I love to hug my server" crowd, the real issue is that you are at the mercy of another company who could cause you a bunch of trouble once your files, data, and processes are operating in its infrastructure.

You might inadvertently violate some policy and find your account is shut down. Or your provider could go out of business and shut off your service. A more likely scenario is that the provider is purchased by another company, which decides that the service you are leveraging is no longer profitable, so it discontinues the service, leaving you to scramble for another solution. The common theme is that there are always risks when you depend on another company that you do not own or control. You need to factor these considerations into the case for cloud computing.

Cost means that while there are clear cost benefits, as discussed in the previous section, there are many instances in which cloud computing is not at all cost effective. In some cases, applications are more costly to operate in the clouds when considering the cost of porting, special features that the application may require, and the fact that on-premise platforms may be less expensive. It is both a benefit and a drawback, so you should always consider cost and do your homework to understand the return on investment of cloud computing (Chapter 4) as related to your specific problem domain.

Openness means that many cloud platforms are proprietary in nature. Once you have written your system using the provider's language and architecture, you may find that moving that system to other cloud providers or back into your enterprise is cost prohibitive. While the cloud providers are working as quickly as they can to come up with a set of standards that will reduce the risk of high porting costs, the safe money is on the fact that this risk will always be somewhat of a trade-off when considering cloud computing—standards or no standards.

Compliance means that those who have to live with audit compliance issues may find that cloud computing providers do not provide the logging and auditing features you need to stay compliant with the many laws that corporate America has to follow. The trend is that cloud computing providers will get better at this, so make sure to understand what your issues are and what the providers are offering as compliance solutions before moving forward.

Service-level agreements record a common understanding about services, priorities, responsibilities, guarantees, and warranties between the cloud provider and the cloud user. Many cloud providers do not offer them, but that will change as larger enterprises with stricter requirements begin to leverage cloud computing. The trend is for cloud computing providers to offer SLAs, but of course they do so by passing the cost of the risk down to the cloud computing platform consumer. It is another issue and cost to consider.

When the Cloud Fits

Now we understand both the benefits and the drawbacks of cloud computing. Let's talk more about whether or not an application or a system is a fit for cloud computing. Keep in mind that this really begins with understanding your own architecture issues and the design patterns of the application. We cover these issues in much more detail in Chapter 10, "Defining Candidate Data, Services, and Processes for the Clouds," and Chapter 11, "Making the Move to Cloud Computing," but it is important that we get a sense of where cloud computing fits before we begin the process of defining our SOA using cloud computing.

Cloud Computing Is a Fit . . .

When the processes, applications, and data are largely independent, or when they are not tightly coupled with other applications or information. The idea is that if they are tightly coupled, they are difficult, if not impossible, to decouple, and thus will not operate independently on a remote platform. If they are loosely coupled, fit is not an issue. Loosely coupled applications are a much better fit for cloud computing.

When the points of integration are well defined, or when there are well-defined points within an application where that application can share data, behavior, and processes. Thus, they are easy to integrate with applications back in the enterprise.

When a lower level of security will work just fine, or when the information to be contained within the cloud computing environment requires a low level of security, and the world will not end if the information somehow got out. Cloud computing systems typically provide "good enough" security, but as we covered earlier in this chapter, they are not yet ready for state secrets.

When the core internal enterprise architecture is healthy, or when you have your own house in order, and thus it is much easier for cloud computing systems to become part of that architecture.

When the Web/Internet is the desired platform, or when you are okay with deploying the user interface within a browser. Today, with the advent of rich Internet applications (RIAs), you have browser-based applications that look and function like native applications.

When cost is an issue, or when there is a clear cost benefit to cloud computing, as discussed earlier. If you are looking to build and deploy an application on the cheap, cloud computing is typically the way to go.

When the applications are new. It is much easier to deploy new applications on cloud platforms than it is to port existing applications there. In the previous section, we discussed some of the issues surrounding the use of proprietary languages and other mechanisms that make moving to cloud computing much more difficult and costly.

Cloud Computing Is Not a Fit . . .

When the processes, applications, and data are largely coupled. If the applications are interdependent, then it is not a good idea to move any of them to a remote cloud platform. They will quickly break. Remember, loosely coupled is good with cloud computing; tightly coupled is bad with cloud computing.

When the points of integration are not well defined, or when there are not good mechanisms in place to synchronize the information and processes hosted on cloud computing providers with those systems that exist within the enterprise. Integrating those sorts of systems in which the interfaces are ill-defined places a lot of risk in the movement toward cloud computing and is not a good fit.

When a high level of security is required, or when security is so much of a risk that you just cannot trust systems that you do not completely control. These types of systems should be rare.

When control is critical to your business. If you cannot afford to outsource a critical component to anybody who is less than 100% reliable, then cloud computing may not be right for you.

When the core internal enterprise architecture needs work. If your enterprise architecture is dysfunctional, then extending it out to cloud-delivered platforms is not a good idea. Get your house in order first, at least to the extent that externalizing systems to cloud resources will not cause harm.

When the application requires a native interface. If you need to leverage native APIs (such as Win32) and browsers are not an option, then cloud computing may not be a good fit.

When cost is an issue. Again, consider the costs holistically. While in many cases cloud computing is a fit, in some cases it is not. We talk more about this in Chapter 4

When the application is legacy. Just as new applications are much easier to move to cloud computing, older or legacy applications are not.

Doing Something Different

There is nothing all that revolutionary about cloud computing. It is more of an evolutionary approach in which some of our key computing platforms are better off on cloud-delivered platforms. In short, we are just extending our way of doing architecture, specifically SOA, to cloud computing platforms. This book reviews some of the issues you need to consider in a shift to cloud computing. More importantly, the book provides a process to define an SOA using cloud computing by making as many right decisions as you can along the way.

It is just about the architecture, and it has always been about the architecture. Cloud computing simply provides those who do SOA—and enterprise architecture—with some cost-effective and innovative architectural options. The core purpose of doing architecture does not change. The core benefits of doing architecture do not change. Cloud computing is about new platforms that are more efficient and effective and that cost less.

CHAPTER 3

Defining the Clouds for the Enterprise

*If the facts don't fit the theory,
change the facts.*

—Albert Einstein

One aspect of this book examines the concept of cloud computing as a mechanism to create a new enterprise architecture that is more efficient and effective than the existing architecture. We are looking to SOA using cloud computing as the way to approach this concept, extending SOA outside of the firewall to the platforms, or architectural options, that cloud computing provides.

While cloud computing is not new, the appearance of new cloud resources makes it much more viable than it was in the past. The trick is to understand what resources are out there, the solution patterns they offer, and how they can fit with your SOA. In other words, understand the options you have for leveraging on-demand or cloud-delivered computing resources and use these resources as a way to make your architecture more efficient and cost effective. That is the endgame here.

By now, you know that computing is a way to leverage computing resources you do not own, accessing those resources over the Internet and paying just for the resources you need, when you need them. However, the types of resources, their value to your enterprise, and their fit within your architecture vary greatly.

In Chapter 2, "Reaching for the Clouds," we talked conceptually about cloud computing, but concepts do not build architectures—solutions do. In this chapter, discuss the component parts of cloud computing introduced in Chapter 1, "Where We Are, How We Got Here, and How to Fix It," and examine each in detail.

As you may recall, cloud computing has the following components:

1. Storage-as-a-service
2. Database-as-a-service
3. Information-as-a-service
4. Process-as-a-service
5. Application-as-a-service
6. Platform-as-a-service
7. Integration-as-a-service
8. Security-as-a-service
9. Management/governance-as-a-service
10. Testing-as-a-service
11. Infrastructure-as-a-service (see Figure 3.1)

This chapter focuses on the advantages and disadvantages of each category of cloud services. The objective is to arm you with enough information to

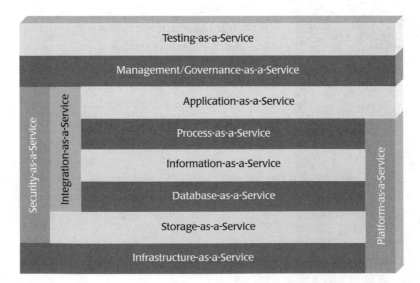

Figure 3.1 Components or categories of cloud computing.

move through the next several chapters where we talk about how to morph your enterprise architecture through SOA using cloud computing to make your IT infrastructure more effective and better aligned with the business. Expect to refer back to this chapter from time to time as you go through the book.

Storage-as-a-Service

Storage-as-a-service, as you may expect, is the ability to leverage storage that physically exists remotely but is logically a local storage resource to any application that requires storage (see Figure 3.2). This is the most primitive component of cloud computing and is leveraged by most of the other cloud computing components.

Using a disk that you access over the Internet is a bit illogical at first. When you think about it, why would some enterprise leverage storage that exists thousands of miles away, as a service, when disk space is so cheap and getting cheaper?

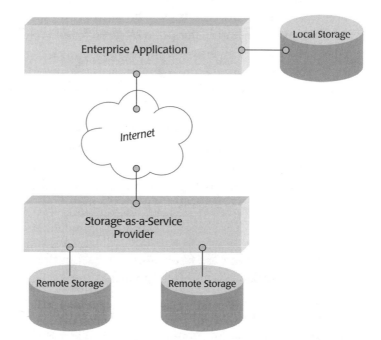

Figure 3.2   Storage-as-a-service allows you to store information on a remote disk drive as if it were local.

There are a few core benefits. First, you can expand the amount of disk space available as you need it and pay only for what you use. You can reduce the amount of disk space—and thereby cost—as the need declines. This makes storage-as-a-service solutions cost effective only for larger volumes of data, typically more than 500 gigabytes, either through direct access or by using the disk as if it were local to your client computer. You can also use the storage-as-a-service provider as a redundant backup for critical files.

Second, you do not have to maintain the hardware. Drives can go down and you do not have to replace them; it is all a part of the service. When compared with an on-premise solution where you have to physically repair the drive, storage-as-a-service removes you from having to deal with that issue.

Finally, the storage-as-a-service provider provides the disaster recovery system for you, and getting back deleted files or entire directories is part of the service. The provider backs up and restores the file system as you require. You do not have to pay someone to handle that task within the data center, and local staff will not have the responsibility of maintaining the storage systems properly.

However, there are some drawbacks to storage-as-a-service. First, you are dependent on the Internet as the mechanism to connect to your storage-as-a-service provider, and if the network goes down, you lose that connection. If a mission-critical need is compromised by a rare and temporary loss of access to your storage, then perhaps storage-as-a-service is not something that makes sense. In many instances, those who leverage storage-as-a-service are surprised to find that they cannot access their shared disk space when not connected to the Internet, such as when on a plane.

Second, performance can be an issue. When compared to on-premise storage, where the disks are physically located near the applications that leverage them, storage-as-a-service does not provide the same performance. Thus, if performance is a critical success factor, storage-as-a-service may not be the approach you want to leverage. Performance is usually about half the speed on a typical Internet connection when compared with a local network. Of course, you can use faster connections, but the cost of implementing a higher speed network connection quickly diminishes the cost savings of storage-as-a-service.

Finally, the cost of the storage-as-a-service provider can be prohibitive when compared with an on-premise solution. While SOA using cloud computing is cost effective in some instances, in many instances it is not. The cost effectiveness of cloud computing is enterprise and domain dependent. For instance, a shared disk in a storage-as-a-service solution would be of high value for a virtual business with a distributed employee base. It would save on hardware and maintenance and would provide easy sharing of disk space as well. However, if the employees or applications are in the same building, the benefits of storage-as-a-service versus on-premise storage solutions are not as compelling.

Database-as-a-Service

Database-as-a-service provides the ability to leverage the services of a remotely hosted database, sharing it with other users and having it logically function as if the database were local. You can self-provision a database, create the tables, load the data, and access the data using the interface provided, all on demand and via cloud computing (see Figure 3.3).

Like storage-as-a-service, database-as-a-service provides access to a resource that you neither own nor host and thus saves you the hardware, software, and maintenance costs. With the self-provisioning capabilities, you can

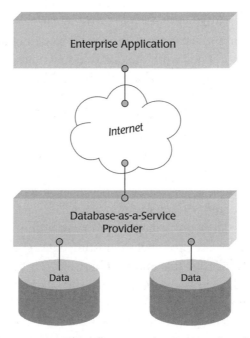

Figure 3.3 Database-as-a-service allows you to access enterprise-grade databases over the Internet.

think about a new database at 8:00 AM and have it running by noon, without buying hardware or software and without even leaving your office. This makes it incredibly easy to provision a database as needed.

Database services include everything that you can do with a local database, such as setting up the tables and the relations among them, adding data, extracting data, and deleting data. Database-as-a-service providers provide not only basic database functions but also brand-specific services such as Oracle, Sybase, and Microsoft, so you can leverage proprietary features if you need them.

An effective database-as-a-service provider should be able to offer database services that appear local in terms of performance and functionality. However, as with the storage-as-a-service offerings, there are always trade-offs.

The benefits of database-as-a-service include, first, the ability to avoid hardware and software costs by leveraging a remote database that you use as you need it and just what you need to use. As many IT professionals already know, database licensing costs are a major part of the software budget, and avoiding those costs will go right to the bottom line.

Second, database maintenance, including backing up and restoring the database and managing users, can be avoided through the use of database-as-a-service. You do not have to focus on the maintenance activities required for a database; you can focus instead on its design and use.

Finally, you can avoid the task of doing upgrades and bug fixes to the database. Many a DBA (database administer) has spent a great deal of time applying patches and fixes to enterprise databases. Using database-as-a-service providers, that activity is handled for you and is transparent to you. You should always have the most current bug-free version of the database engine, since it is centrally updated on the cloud computing site and nothing needs to be distributed.

Database-as-a-service has a few drawbacks as well. First, there are legal, compliancy, and privacy issues around data, and in some instances, leveraging remote databases is illegal and/or not within compliance for some types of data. You must check before hosting data remotely, but in most cases, remote hosting is just fine and should meet your security requirements.

Second, security can be an issue when using database-as-a-service. When you require complete security, the use of remote databases that you do not control or secure may be contraindicated, depending on the type of data you place in those databases. However, there is no reason you cannot have your data exist securely on a database-as-a-service cloud offering if you leverage the right approach to security for your SOA and the right security technology. You need to work closely with your database-as-a-service provider and consider your own requirements to determine the best approach to secure your database.

Third, many of the interfaces offered by database-as-a-service providers are proprietary in nature and thus can be difficult to leverage from applications that need to access the data. While many cloud computing providers are moving toward standard interfaces, you need to understand and test their interfaces and/or APIs.

Finally, some database-as-a-service providers offer only a subset of the capabilities found in traditional on-premise enterprise databases. You may find that you are missing features and functions required by the enterprise applications. For example, stored procedures and triggers may not be supported in the same manner as in on-premise databases, or they may be proprietary, and thus difficult to port if you need to move off the database-as-a-service provider at some point in the future.

Information-as-a-Service

Information-as-a-service refers to the ability to consume any type of remotely hosted information—stock price information, address validation, credit reporting, for example—through a well-defined interface such as an API (see Figure 3.4). Over a thousand sources of information can be found these days, most of them listed at www.programmableweb.com. While they typically "serve up" information using standard Web Services APIs, some use proprietary interfaces. Therefore, as you must for database-as-a-service, you need to consider the interfaces offered by information-as-a-service providers.

Typically, APIs function like this:

```
GetSSNName(SSN_Number);
```

or

```
GetSSNName(333-33-3333);
```

with the return of

```
"John H. Smith"
```

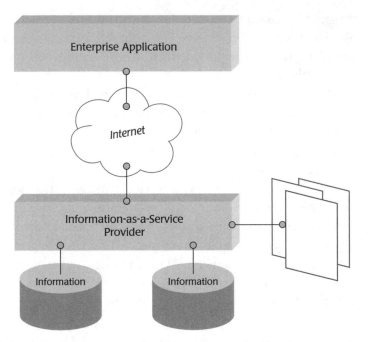

Figure 3.4   Information-as-a-service allows any application to access any type of information using an API.

Pretty simple. But that is just one type of API. Others are more complex, perhaps returning complete structures with information bound to those structures.

You can leverage a wide variety of Web APIs these days, including APIs for social networking sites like Twitter and Facebook, for business statistics, for stock quotes, and the list goes on. As far as cloud computing categories go, information-as-a-service is the most eclectic.

We use information through these APIs for several reasons, including the ability to mix and match a variety of information from many different sources through a single application or mashup. We can get stock quotes from one information-as-a-service provider, census data from another, and Dun & Bradstreet (D&B) information from a third. The idea is that it is much cheaper to leverage information that other people maintain and host than it is to host it yourself.

Those charged with creating an SOA using cloud computing must understand the value of Web APIs and must have the skills to produce a good-faith estimate as to what that value is. In essence, they must determine an approach to define the return on investment (ROI) and then determine the ROI itself. Let's explore these concepts, focusing on the costs, the benefits, and the business case in the context of leveraging information-as-a-service, or Web APIs.

The core value of leveraging Web APIs is that you do not have to incur the cost of creating or hosting the API or the information it abstracts. While most hang their value hat on that truth, there is indeed cost to leveraging an outside API:

- Cost of binding APIs into applications or processes, including abstracting an API to fit an application or process.
- Cost of inefficiencies brought about by the use of the API, such as downtime, or decreased speed.
- Cost of ongoing maintenance as APIs and applications change.
- Cost of the API service itself, typically per use.

Normally, the cost to bind an API to an application is not significant. However, in many instances, the API does not provide the exact function the application requires. Thus, some additional programming needs to be completed. And since you bind an application to a remote resource of a network, you have to account for the remote resource—the network—being down from time to time. Furthermore, there is always ongoing maintenance and the cost of the service itself. So,

Onetime cost = cost of binding and abstraction
Ongoing cost = cost of downtime + ongoing maintenance + cost of the API service

As an example, consider a simple phone number verification service remotely hosted:

Onetime cost = $1,000
Ongoing cost (per month) = $100 + $200 + $100

The onetime cost is $1,000, and the ongoing cost is $400 per month. Together they equal the cost of leveraging an API. We use these figures when we look at benefits. So, while the costs are typically hidden and not significant, they do exist.

The larger issue around ROI and Web APIs is the value of leveraging versus creating a Web API and maintaining the back-end data yourself. We need to look at how much it would cost us if the API did not exist and we had to create it ourselves.

Again, functionality will vary greatly from API to API, but using our simple phone number verification service example, we can consider how much that API would cost were we to build it and host it ourselves. Generally speaking,

> Onetime cost = cost of designing, building, and testing the API
> Ongoing cost = cost of downtime + ongoing maintenance + cost of the data subscription

Again, as an example, a simple phone number verification service remotely hosted might involve the following costs:

Onetime cost = $20,000
Ongoing cost (per month) = $200 + $1,000 + $500

The onetime cost is $20,000, and the ongoing is $1,700 per month, so for this particular case, we can look at the value of leveraging a Web API as follows:

	Onetime Cost	Ongoing Cost
Build and Host	$20,000	$1,700
Web API	$1,000	$400
Savings	$19,000	$1,300

On a yearly basis, that would be that would be $20,300 to the bottom line in the first year and $1,300 thereafter. Time-to-market costs are not considered here, but leveraging a prebuilt API will clearly provide better time-to-market.

Keep in mind that, typically, dozens of APIs are leveraged at the same time, thus multiplying the value. Also, keep in mind that each API has its own unique value to a particular business.

While the technology acquisition and maintenance costs are compelling, we must consider the larger and more difficult to determine "soft costs" of leveraging an API—or the value that the API brings to the business in terms of more sales, better customer satisfaction, and better employee morale.

Here is where we find the most value from leveraging a Web API. While there is indeed a cost savings in using a remotely hosted API versus supporting the same process on-premise, the service could be something that provides much more value.

For instance, the ability for the sales department to do a D&B lookup while on the phone with a particular customer provides critical customer information that will assist in closing a sale and prioritizing sales costs. The ability to do an instant credit check while completing a sale, without having to leverage a separate system and keep the customer waiting, benefits the salesperson, the customer, and thus the business.

We take a closer look at how to create a business case for cloud computing and SOA using cloud computing in Chapter 4. The use case described here is a starting point for understanding the value of cloud computing versus on-premise computing. Of course, the ROI that it will bring to your enterprise is depends completely on what you do and how you do it. The fit for cloud computing is not always there, but you always do your analysis with an open mind.

Why the Most Popular Web APIs, or Information-as-a-Service Offerings, Are Free

"You get what you pay for"—but that does not seem to be the case with the new cloud computing movement, specifically with Web APIs. Some of the best services out there do not require a credit card number, and that trend will continue until greater numbers of the available Web APIs have normalized. That is going to be awhile.

For example, the GeoNames Web API, from geonames.org, is a geographical database that can be downloaded for free under a creative commons attribution license. The database contains over 8 million geographical names and provides a broad range of information on each, from its population and form of government to its topology to its road and railway systems and more. It contains 6.3 million unique features, 2.2 million populated places, and 1.8 million alternate names of places.

However, if you do not want to download this data, and most of us have no need to, the data is accessible free of charge through a number of Web Services. Geonames.org already serves up to over 11 million Web Service requests per day, and all for no subscription fees. There are already over 40 mashups that leverage this API, as well as those who leverage it for any number of enterprises or Web applications out there.

continued

How will money be made from providing APIs for free? You have to consider that most of the content on the Web is free to the browser user. Business models are driven in other ways, such as by advertising revenue. In other cases, sites that offer data for free to the browsers are simply providing the data using another mechanism. Thus, there are more ways to leverage the data directly within other applications or mashups. It is logical to expect that most of the more popular data-as-a-service APIs will remain free or available at a very low fee. After all, while the use of Web APIs expands, the key is adoption and leveraging, and the money will come down the road for those who find their APIs pervasively embedded within enterprises or clouds, through enterprise usage fees—in essence, the same way those who create freeware make money today.

Eventually, you will see fees for information delivered via APIs that you would pay to see within a browser. Moreover, there are complex business services and data, delivered as APIs, that may actually have to charge large fees right away considering the limited audience and the costs of development and support. However, they will typically be much cheaper than having to develop those services and maintain that data yourself. We do not see many of these types of services yet, but as the world of the nonvisual Web expands, more of them will show up on the market.

Should the possibility of future fees affect your development efforts? A better question might be, How did the possibility of future fees related to expanding your business onto the Internet affect your business? Be aware of their potential, but also be aware of the benefits.

You also need to consider proprietary issues—APIs that cause "lock-in," or the inability to leverage other APIs in its place because the interface it leverages does not exist anywhere else. As with database-as-a-service offerings, you have to consider the downsides to proprietary interfaces that do not allow you to easily move to other APIs.

Process-as-a-Service

Process-as-a-service refers to a remote resource that can bind many resources together, either hosted within the same cloud computing resource or remotely, to create business processes (see Figure 3.5). An example would

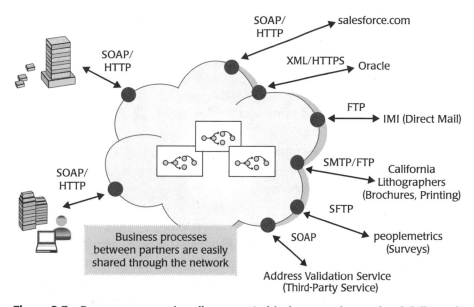

Figure 3.5 Process-as-a-service allows you to bind on-premise or cloud-delivered resources together to form business solutions.

be to create a business process that defines how to process an invoice on remote cloud-delivered systems and then have that process invoke any number of cloud-based or on-premise services to form the business process. The SOA gains the value of agility because processes are easier to change than applications.

We cover processes in more detail in Chapter 7, "Working from Your Processes to the Clouds." For now, it is enough to understand that processes are meta-applications that bind many services and information together to form a business solution. Because they follow a configuration rather than a programmatic approach, it is often easier to create and change processes using a graphical interface than to write new programs.

Process-as-a-service provides a mechanism to bind other resources together to form a solution. While your information and APIs may be hosted within a cloud provider, or perhaps on-premise, you would leverage this service to abstract and bind these resources together to form a business solution, such as processing a sale or shipping a product.

You can think of processes as a sequence of events that must occur in a certain order, leveraging any number of services and portions of data. For example,

Process "Ship Product"
1. Transmit order to warehouse.
2. Process shipping provider.
3. Price shipping.
4. Turn over to shipping provider.
5. Track shipment.
6. Report to customer.

Each step above includes services called by the process, but the services themselves are not processes. Processes provide control instructions about how to do something using many resources that can exist on-premise or in the clouds. Processes can span a single enterprise or, more often, many enterprises when dealing with process-as-a-service (see Figure 3.6).

Process engines are really nothing new, although the existence of process engines on demand is. As we move forward with cloud computing, the use of process engines to leverage and manage any number of local and remote services to form them into business solutions will be an important component to cloud computing and to SOA using cloud computing.

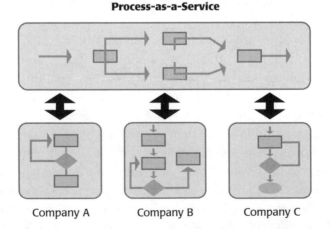

Process-as-a-Service

Company A   Company B   Company C

Figure 3.6 Process-as-a-service allows you to create common processes that span many companies, cloud services, and on-premise services.

Application-as-a-Service

Application-as-a-service, also known as software-as-a-service, is any application delivered over the platform of the Web to an end user, typically leveraging the application through a browser. While many associate application-as-a-service with enterprise applications, such as Salesforce SFA, office automation applications are indeed applications-as-a-service as well, including Google Docs, Gmail, and Google Calendar. They typically offer

- A user interface.
- Predefined application behavior.
- Predefined data.
- Support for any number of client platforms, since they run through the browser.

Application-as-a-service was really the first drive into modern cloud computing, but it is based on the more traditional time-sharing model from years past whereby many users shared one application and one computer. The differences are that we use a Web browser, not a terminal, and the applications are typically sold by subscription, not by time. Some are free of charge and obtain revenue through advertising or in other ways.

The advantage of application-as-a-service is the ability to leverage an enterprise-class application without having to buy and install enterprise software. Thus, business functionality typically only available to those who could afford SAP, Oracle Financials, and other larger packaged systems are available to any business user for a small subscription fee. Indeed, Salesforce.com became a multibillion dollar business using this model, and other application-as-a-service providers are catching up quickly, including many providing specialized applications for human resources, logistics management, and trade risk management, to name just a few.

Application-as-a-Service and APIs

Many application-as-a-service providers offer API access to their internal behaviors and data. Their customers need programmatic access to the application behavior and the information for any number of purposes, such as

continued

integration, or the ability to leverage services from an application-as-a-service provider for their on-premise enterprise applications.

Thus, while an application-as-a-service is indeed an application, the ability to provide API access also places some applications-as-a-service in the category of process-as-a-service or information-as-a-service, or both. Keep that in mind.

In addition to the larger business application-as-a-service, there are also the office automation applications-as-a-service, including e-mail, document management, word processing, spreadsheets, and other productivity applications delivered through a browser. Google provides these applications for free, as do a few other providers. Some charge a small subscription fee.

The advantage of leveraging office automation applications-as-a-service are really around cost and convenience. Cost, because it is typically free. However, you can use Sun's Open Office open source office automation software on your desktop, which is also free, just to be fair. Convenience, since any computer with a browser can become your personal workspace with access to your documents and e-mail. So, you could be just as productive at an Internet café using a public computer as you would be at work.

The Intercloud and Cloud Interoperability

The big push right now is around interoperability among cloud providers, or the notion of cloud providers offering built-in communications to one another and application and data portability among providers. Core to this concept is a buzzword: *Intercloud.*

Although this is one of those new topics that is widely defined, the Intercloud is really the concept of allowing cloud providers to exchange information and behavior in support of those who use the cloud. Like the Internet, they want to connect many different things together and provide a standard mechanism for doing so.

This is important for a few reasons. First, it puts the responsibility for communicating among providers on the providers, not on the users. Second, it provides a foundation for interoperability that, to date, has been pretty ad hoc.

Finally, it reduces the price point of cloud computing, and considering the previous two points, cost is the core selling point of the clouds.

Cloud providers see the value of promoting interoperability even though many would love to have the customer locked in. However, in these days when open source is a much better sell than proprietary features, cloud vendors could find that providing interoperability gets many enterprises off the fence and moving toward the clouds.

The success of interoperability within the cloud providers' realms will depend on their ability to stop building features and start building for interoperability. With the huge land grab going on right now, that is easy to talk about but tougher to do. At the end of the day, cloud users will have to insist on openness, as they did in the world of SOA and other architectural shifts in thinking.

This could very well be one of those times when everyone talks a good game and pays dues into some organization promoting standards, but the solution continues to be proprietary because of the cost and latency that the cloud providers will have to suffer when coordinating with their competition. Again, end users will have to make it a core criteria for provider selection. As with anything, money talks.

Platform-as-a-Service

Platform-as-a-service is a complete platform, including application development, interface development, database development, storage, and testing, delivered through a remotely hosted platform to subscribers. Based on the traditional time-sharing model, modern platform-as-a-service providers offer the ability to create enterprise-class applications for use locally or on demand for a small subscription price or for free.

You can think of platform-as-a-service as one-stop shopping for those looking to build and deploy applications. Platform-as-a-service provides self-contained platforms with everything you need for application development and operational hosting. Platforms such as Google App Engine and Force.com (part of Salesforce.com) are popular ways to approach application development on the cloud.

Core to the platform-as-a-service notion are a few major components: design, development, deployment, integration, storage, and operations.

Design is the ability to design your application and user interfaces.

Development is the ability to design, develop, and test applications right out of the platform, on demand, using development tools that are delivered on demand. We have seen the Salesforce.com Apex language provide these services, with a few smaller players providing similar capabilities.

Deployment is the ability to test, bundle, and deliver the platform-as-a-service–created applications. This means hosting the applications, typically accessing them visually, through a browser, or as Web services.

Integration is the ability to integrate the applications developed on your platform-as-a-service provider with software-as-a-service applications or applications that may exist within your enterprise.

Storage, the ability to provide persistence for the application, means an on-demand database or on-demand file storage.

Finally, *operations* is the ability to run the application over a long period of time, dealing with backup, restore, exception handling, and other things that add value to operations.

Platform-as-a-service is going to deliver only a subset of the existing features and functions most of us look for in a platform, but it will deliver enough value to be interesting as a service. Platforms are costly, and the ability to create a platform through a subscription service is compelling. Many professionals in the Global 2000 companies see platform-as-a-service as a way to develop, deploy, and maintain critical applications on the cheap.

When Considering Platform-as-a-Service, Watch Out for Lock-In

While platform-as-a-service is a popular way to do application development and deployment in the clouds, many providers offer only proprietary development languages and other application development and deployment technology that make it very difficult to move your application from a platform-as-a-service to another platform. While interoperability standards are under development, for now, you should always be aware that platform-as-a-service lock-in could be a drawback.

The advantage of platform-as-a-service is that you can access a complete enterprise-class development environment at a low cost and build complete enterprise applications, from the data to the user interface. The disadvantage is that many of the platform-as-a-service vendors leverage proprietary programming languages and interfaces; thus, once your application is there, it may be difficult to move it to an on-premise server or another platform-as-a-service provider.

Integration-as-a-Service

Integration-as-a-service is the ability to deliver a complete integration stack from the cloud, including interfacing with applications, semantic mediation, flow control, and integration design. In essence, integration-as-a-service includes most of the features and functions found within traditional EAI (enterprise application integration) technology but delivered as a service.

Integration is a tough problem to solve, and integration on demand does not make that any easier. The core notion is that you link up to many information systems, either at the data or behavior level, and abstract information and/or behavior from those systems to be delivered with one or many systems, either within the same enterprise or within companies.

There are many books on integration, so we do not get into it too much here. However, any integration engine, on-premise or in the cloud, has to support some basic functions, including (to name just a few):

- Transformation
- Routing
- Interface
- Logging

Transformation means that you can convert the information semantics from one system to the information semantics of another system, so the target system can receive information in a format it understands.

Routing means that information is routed to the correct systems on the basis of predefined logic (called intelligent routing).

Interface means that you can connect into the source or target systems using whatever interface they expose.

Logging means that you can log all integration activities, such as messages flowing in and out, as well as other events.

The advantage of integration-as-a-service is that you can access pretty pricy integration software functionality for the price of a rental agreement. Moreover, many of the integration-on-demand providers have very sophisticated software delivered through a browser that leverage the new rich Internet application technology such as AJAX.

The downside is that there are many firewall mediation issues to deal with. Many systems you may want to integrate do not have Port 80–compliant interfaces and protocols, meaning they cannot speak outside of the firewall to the remote, on-demand integration server. Thus, many integration-on-demand providers leverage software that has to exist behind the firewall to mediate the differences in the local, native interfaces and turn them into something that can be sent outside of the firewall, typically Web Services that leverage Port 80–compliant Simple Object Access Protocol (SOAP). Thus, you end up with an on-premise footprint that diminishes the value of an integration-on-demand solution.

Security-as-a-Service

Security-as-a-service, as you may have guessed, is the ability to deliver core security services remotely over the Internet. While the security services provided today are often rudimentary, more sophisticated services, such as identity management, are becoming available.

Security-as-a-service is a tough sell considering that security is typically a weak point of cloud computing. Providing security on demand seems like an unnatural act. However, there are times when security delivered out of the cloud makes sense, such as for securing a cluster of cloud resources you are leveraging within your enterprise or even between enterprises. Thus, you can enforce security hierarchies between physical organizations out of the cloud or perhaps have cloud-delivered on-demand encryption services or identity management solutions.

The downside is rather obvious, considering that most look at security as something that needs to be controlled and thus not outsourced. However, as time goes on and security on demand becomes more sophisticated, and as more corporate data and applications reside in the clouds, then there will be an uptake in security-as-a-service.

Management/Governance-as-a-Service

Management/governance-as-a-service is any on-demand service that provides the ability to manage one or more cloud services, typically simple things such topology, resource utilization, virtualization, and uptime management. Governance systems, such as the ability to enforce defined policies on data and services, are becoming available as well. We cover governance in great detail in Chapter 8, "Bringing Governance to the Clouds."

Much the same as with security on demand, this aspect of cloud computing is slow on the uptake. Most enterprises like to control management and governance. However, as more applications and data are outsourced, it may make sense to manage and govern those resources from the clouds as well.

Testing-as-a-Service

Testing-as-a-service is the ability to test local or cloud-delivered systems using remotely hosted testing software and services. It should be noted that while a cloud service requires testing unto itself, testing-as-a-service systems have the ability to test other cloud applications, Web sites, and internal enterprise systems, and they do not require a hardware or software footprint within the enterprise.

The advantages of testing-as-a-service include the ability to avoid purchasing test servers and testing software. Moreover, in many respects, testing, either on-premise or in the clouds, is better done through a testing service that connects to those applications over the Internet, since many real-life users will do the same thing. Thus, if you are looking to test a Web site or a Web-delivered application, testing-as-a-service is actually more logical than testing on-premise in many instances.

The downsides are the ones you might expect. Many of those who build and deploy applications like to control their testing environments and would not dream of leveraging testing servers and software that they do not own or host. Again, as more applications are rehosted in the cloud, testing-as-a-service will become more of an accepted paradigm.

Infrastructure-as-a-Service

Infrastructure-as-a-service is really data center-as-a-service, or the ability to access computing resources remotely. In essence, you lease a physical server that is yours to do with what you will and that for all practical purposes is your data center, or at least part of a data center. The difference with this approach versus more mainstream cloud computing is that instead of using an interface and a metered service, you get access to the entire machine and the software on that machine. In short, it is less packaged.

We defined database-as-a-service, storage-as-a-service, and so on, as separate categories of cloud computing. Infrastructure-as-a-service can provide all of them, including database, storage, governance, application development, application processing, security, and more. Anything that can be found in a traditional data center can be delivered as an infrastructure-as-a-service. The overlapping feature of infrastructure-as-a-service and the other cloud computing services can make this a bit confusing.

The advantage of infrastructure-as-a-service is that you can access very expensive data center resources through a rental arrangement and thus preserve capital for the business. Moreover, somebody is there to manage the physical machines for you, including replacement of downed disk drives and correction of any networking issues.

The disadvantage is that there is typically less granular on-demand expandability of the resource. With database-as-a-service and storage-as-a-service, you just purchase additional capability as you need it and as much as you need. However, many infrastructure-as-a-service providers require that you lease an entire server for a defined amount of time. Thus, the whole selling point of adjusting your cloud resources to meet your exact needs kind of goes out the door.

Next Steps

Keep in mind that the components of cloud computing will change over time as our thinking and the market evolves. However, the general patterns presented in this chapter will be relatively consistent as cloud computing evolves; just the names and the features may change a bit. What is most important is that you recognize and understand the resources you have to work with to change your enterprise architecture by leveraging cloud computing.

The next steps are about how to change your enterprise architecture to incorporate SOA using cloud computing. We look at how to approach your enterprise architecture by understanding what you have and how cloud computing and SOA may improve it.

CHAPTER 4

Making the Business Case for Clouds

Money is better than poverty,
if only for financial reasons.
—Woody Allen (1935–)

You might think that cloud computing would always be more cost effective than on-premise computing. However, the value that cloud computing brings to your enterprise depends on many variables and dynamics of your business. Therefore, like anything that means change, you need to work the business case first to see the ultimate worth of this approach.

The forces at work here include strategic and tactical issues that should be analyzed, including the ability to shift risk to cloud computing providers, the ability to drive down operating costs, the ability to fix inefficiencies within the existing architecture, and the value all of that brings. The problem is that most enterprises do not analyze these business opportunities holistically and thus make many mistakes when building the larger business case. If we're going to be honest about it, enterprise architects are notoriously bad at creating business cases.

The purpose of this chapter is to bring a bit of business sense to cloud computing and examine its effect on enterprise IT, sometimes good, sometimes not so good. This is really a plan to create a plan, or the ability to objectively determine what the real benefits are of all this change and thus to sell this change to those who drive the business.

It is one thing to say that cloud computing makes life better because everybody says it does; it is another to say that cloud computing will make this company more than $50 million over the next 5 years. The ability to make money will always outsell something cool and popular. Keep that in mind as you create the business case and sell cloud computing to your executive team.

Defining the Holistic Value

While most in IT think cloud computing is really about the ability to save operational costs, that may or may not be the case, depending on your enterprise or problem domain. There are many dimensions to consider here, including

- Ongoing operational cost reduction.
- The value of preserving capital.
- The value of upsizing on demand.
- The value of downsizing on demand.
- The value of shifting the risk.
- The value of agility.
- The value of reuse.
- The value of coolness.

Let's explore each.

Operational Cost Reduction

We all know that cloud computing is cheap . . . okay, cheaper . . . okay, it can be cheap. Thus, it is a good idea to figure out the actual cost reductions that cloud computing can bring to your enterprise IT. The trick is to figure out not only how much money can be saved but how much it will cost to save that money. Follow me here.

Let's say you decided that cloud computing is the way to go for a major enterprise application and that the costs of an on-premise instance versus a cloud computing instance are as follows:

On-Premise

Hardware	$100,000
Software	$100,000 for license, $20,000 per year software maintenance
Maintenance	$200,000 per year for people to work the system
Data Center	$50,000 per year

We assume an enterprise application package with some customization. Development from scratch would cost more. Based on experience, our estimated costs are very conservative. Thus, we can say that over 5 years, the cash burn will be $1,530,000:

Year 1	$450,000
Year 2	$270,000
Year 3	$270,000
Year 4	$270,000
Year 5	$270,000

Pretty expensive. Now let's look at the cloud computing options, using the same 5-year cost horizon.

Cloud Computing

Hardware	$0
Software	$10,000 per month subscription
Maintenance	$0
Data Center	$0

Over 5 years, the cash burn will be $600,000 (see Figure 4.1):

Year 1	$120,000
Year 2	$120,000
Year 3	$120,000
Year 4	$120,000
Year 5	$120,000

This assumes a pretty simple application-on-demand scenario. The cost will be more complex with a cloud computing solution that may leverage a variety of cloud providers, since you have to pay the people who make those work and play well together and for application development. This is just an example, and we use this case study for other concepts presented in this chapter.

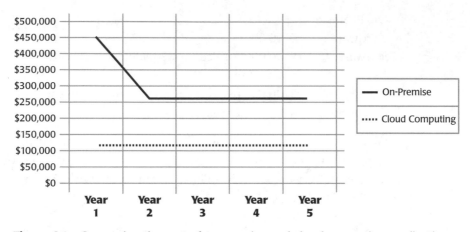

Figure 4.1   Comparing the cost of on-premise and cloud computing applications.

IT Costs Are Always Complex

As you go through this chapter, keep in mind that simple cost models for IT operations rarely represent real life. You have to consider all costs holistically, including hard costs such as the cost of acquisition and operations as well as the harder-to-determine costs. For example, what to do with the existing hardware and software you have already paid for, and the data center space you have already leased—that's a cost. The risks around leveraging a platform you do not own—that's a cost. The risk that prices on cloud computing services could go up in the future—that's a cost. You get the idea.

Also, you have to consider the soft or hidden costs such as the strategic value of bringing an application to market quicker by leveraging a cloud computing solution versus an on-premise solution. There could be a huge business benefit in market timing. You must also consider the ability to service your customers and partners better using cloud computing–based systems than you can using on-premise systems.

The point is that simple cost models can make a strong case for moving to cloud computing or leveraging on-premise systems, but they often do not include the majority of costs and benefits you need to consider. Creating an accurate business case means understanding and modeling many elements, some easy to determine and some more difficult. The cost model will be complex, but it needs to be complex to be useful.

It appears that the cloud solution is much more cost effective when look-ing at the core analysis. However, there are other things you need to consider that are often left out of the model: integration, network impact, and com-pliance, just to list a few.

These other expenses are required for several reasons: First, you gener-ally need to sync the information back to the existing on-premise enterprise applications and therefore need to factor in the cost for the integration solu-tion to make that happen in an ongoing manner. That will run about $5,000 per month, per information system, with another $5,000 in human costs to maintain it, as a rule of thumb. However, it is largely domain dependent, so be sure to do your own integration solution cost analysis.

Second, you need look at the network impact. For the most part, unless you are looking to move terabytes of data, this is pretty cheap. However, you must consider it. It is a good idea to model the impact on the network and model up through the transaction loads for years 1 through 5.

Finally, the costs of compliance, such as the ability to build in auditing processes, including logging, and to support privacy regulations, such as those created by the government, should be considered as well.

So, let's add in $5,000 monthly for integration and $3,000 monthly for compliance—not untypical. Again, you have to analyze these costs for your own problem domain.

Over 5 years, the cash burn will look like this:

Year 1	$216,000
Year 2	$216,000
Year 3	$216,000
Year 4	$216,000
Year 5	$216,000

The total cost will be $ 1,080,000 over 5 years. Still better, but with the addi-tional and less visible costs built in, the gap has closed a bit (see Figure 4.2). Of course, within some problem domains, both integration and compliance may not be required, but other costs may be required; this is just an example.

Even with these costs considered, the cloud-delivered solution, generally speaking, will be more cost effective for a problem domain with a small num-ber of cost variables. Of course, as we pointed out in the previous Book Blog, IT cost models are typically much more complex and must consider issues that are dependent on the special needs of the business; they are all a bit different.

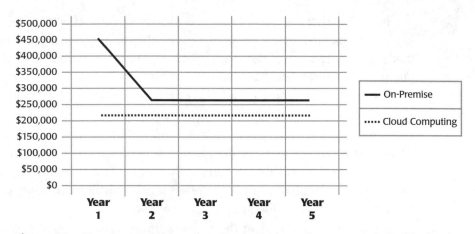

Figure 4.2 You must consider all costs when comparing on-premise with cloud computing. Many of these costs are less obvious and depend on the business.

Thus, the purpose here is to get you into the habit of considering all costs, holistically, when it comes to comparing on-premise to cloud computing, considering that we are looking at cloud computing as an architectural option for our SOA. You will find that within the world of cloud computing, we forget or do not understand many of the costs involved in leveraging cloud computing versus more traditional approaches, since cloud computing, at least using the newer technology, is fairly new to us. Just to make sure you have the general checklist, they include the following:

1. Integration
2. Compliance
3. Bandwidth
4. Storage
5. Recovery service
6. Humans needed
7. Outage management
8. Domain- or enterprise-specific issues
9. Rise in subscription costs
10. Security
11. Capital costs

Make sure you consider these items when costing out a cloud computing solution. Some will not make much of a difference, some are very significant. These costs are very enterprise and domain dependent.

Preserving Capital

What the heck is capital? As defined by Wikipedia, it is

> any liquid medium or mechanism that represents wealth, or other styles of capital. It is, however, usually purchasing power in the form of money available for the production or purchasing of goods, et cetera. Capital can also be obtained by producing more than what is immediately required and saving the surplus.[1]

In other words, it is money in the bank that allows the business to run. The more money we have in the bank, the more we can purchase things for the core business, such as inventory that can be sold or new plant equipment that will save the company money during production. It is good to keep as much capital as possible on hand to invest in the business instead of into infrastructure such as data centers, hardware, and software.

Considering the example case study, if we need to conserve capital, then cloud computing seems to be the way to go. We pay as we use the service, there is no hardware and/or software to buy, and we can keep the money in the bank for other purposes. There is a clear value that you can assign to the preservation of capital, which is largely dependent on the business and needs to be considered with this analysis.

The benefits of preserving capital are significant. Startups can launch an entire company with almost no IT expense, new divisions can be created with little IT capital investment, and there is no need to reinvest in hardware, software, and data center resources as the business scales up. Moreover, there is no reason to keep those capital resources around as the business scales down. With cloud computing, it is just a matter of paying more, or less, for the use of the service. We can call this the value of upsizing and downsizing on demand.

---

1. http://en.wikipedia.org/wiki/Financial_capital

Upsizing On Demand

Core to the ability to preserve capital is the ability to upsize your IT infrastructure on demand, or simply pay more money for additional computing capacity. Many cloud computing providers call this being elastic, or having the ability to grow or contract to accommodate the business. There are a few terms to consider here:

- Service tiers
- Existing resources
- Ability to scale

Service tiers are offered by some cloud computing providers: for example, you can purchase some capacity for $1,000 a month, the next tier up is $2,500, and the next one up is $5,000. Therefore, you must consider the cost of service tiers compared to more granular billing methods.

You have to consider the contracts as well. While some are monthly, some are yearly, and some are both. Thus, many of those contracts can drive a commitment that may not be right for the enterprise. Make sure to read the service agreement carefully before selecting a cloud computing provider, and make sure you understand what will happen if you move from that provider, increase processing, or decrease processing (discussed shortly). Do this before selecting the provider and signing the agreement.

Existing resources refers to the fact that you may have some computing capacity around in the data center that is already bought and paid for, and thus using those resources should be considered. However, you also need to consider the costs of development and maintenance, which are typically where the real costs come in. The trick is to understand that your CIO will probably ask about those resources during the cloud computing discussions, and you need to have a well-thought-out answer. The answer could be that moving to cloud computing is not cost justified, considering the existing investment in hardware, software, and data center space.

Ability to scale is the ability for the cloud computing provider to actually provide the capacity you require to support the additional computing resources you will need. While most can scale up to your needs, there are some that will not be able to handle the additional load no matter how much money you pay them. You need to determine that up front.

Downsizing On Demand

Just as you must for upsizing on demand, you must consider what it will take to reduce computing capacity and dollars paid. In essence, what does it take to scale down if you no longer need the computing resource and want to reduce costs as well? There are a few things to consider here:

- Service agreements
- Existing resources
- Ability to contract

Service agreements are the agreements signed with a cloud computing provider regarding changing the agreement to reduce the capacity and the spending. While some allow you to freely change the use of the service, some, like cell phone contracts, do not let you out of the agreement, and thus you might reduce use but the cost will remain the same. You must look at the service agreement closely before signing.

Existing resources, as we stated previously, involves the need to consider the existing underutilized computing resources.

Ability to contract is not as much of an issue as the ability to scale, but work with your cloud provider to make sure there are no issues should you need to scale down.

Shifting the Risk

Another core value of cloud computing is the ability to shift the risk from your enterprise to the cloud computing provider. Because it is up to the cloud provider to handle the computing processing load and you pay by use, you can reduce the risk of running out of capacity to support your customers and core business processes. That risk functionally shifts to the cloud provider, who is better suited to accept the risk.

So, while you reduce your risk as computing needs go up, you also reduce the risk that you have purchased excess capacity that you do not need. In short, you have outsourced your data center to those who will manage it, keep it healthy, and charge you only for what you use over time. The business (yours) that is not in business to provide computing resources can exit from the risk around that business and transfer that risk to cloud providers who are in the computing resources business.

Perhaps it is better to use an example. Let's say you are supporting an inventory management system and you leverage cloud computing resources for database-as-a-service and platform-as-a-service. In this example, you avoid the cost of data center–bound resources, and more importantly, the cost of the risk. By leveraging cloud computing resources, you avoid the investment in a set of on-premise computing resources that have two major attributes: First, they require a specific amount of capital investment for hardware and software; second, they have an upper limit in scalability from the point where you need to purchase additional resources to scale up processing to meet the needs of the business.

In Figure 4.3, you can see that the investment of $500,000 in hardware gets you to a specific number of transactions per day, and then you have to invest again to support the increasing load as transaction volumes increase. You have excess capacity you are paying for, and you are taking on the risk. Indeed, you always have to keep additional capacity on hand in order to handle the peak transaction processing loads. This does not consider the disruptive nature of purchasing, configuring, installing, and testing new hardware and software.

In this scenario, there is the risk that, for the amount of capital committed, it will provide either more capacity than is required for a specific period of time or not enough capacity for a particular period of time. Either way, you are running a risk.

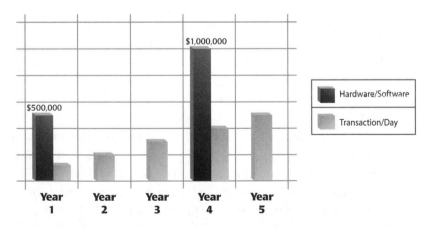

Figure 4.3   When using an on-premise approach, you have to purchase hardware and software to support the current processing load, and then reinvest in the future in order to scale. The risk is on you.

When leveraging a cloud computing resource or resources, the risk is usually reduced because you leverage only the capacity you need, and the cost adjusts according to the capacity you use (see Figure 4.4). At a lower capacity, you are not wasting money by having idle computing resources around, nor are you risking that you will not have the resources to scale, since the cloud computing resources are on demand.

Risk of Being Dumped

You can indeed shift the risk to the cloud computing provider, but in many instances, there is another risk to consider: that the cloud computing provider will simply stop providing you with cloud computing services. This leaves you looking for other options and perhaps damages your business.

While cloud computing providers are not in the business of dumping customers, outside forces such as an acquisition could take place, and the purchasing company may decide that a particular cloud computing platform is unprofitable and must be shut down. Or, the cloud computing provider may go out of business for any number of reasons. Or, it may decide that you have violated some policy and discontinue your service.

It is important to note that the risks go in two directions: (1) shifting the risk to the cloud computing provider around your need to expand and contract IT in support of the business, and (2) accepting the risk that the cloud

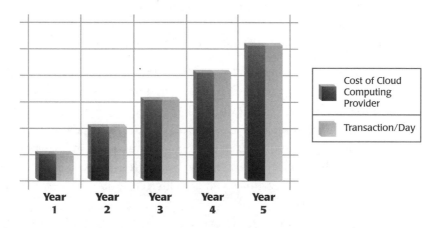

Figure 4.4 When leveraging a cloud computing resource, you can scale up as you need to scale up, thereby putting the risk on the cloud computing provider, not on the enterprise.

computing provider could suddenly discontinue service. There are cost/benefit trade-offs to be consider here, so make sure you dial both the upside and the downside risks into your business case.

Agility and Reuse

Agility and reuse are part of the value of cloud computing, and each has its own benefit to enterprise architecture. First is the ability to save development dollars through reuse of services and applications. (We talk about services in Chapter 6, "Working from Your Services to the Clouds." For now, it is helpful to note that many services make up an application instance.) These services may have been built inside or outside of the company, and the more services that are reusable from system to system, the more ROI is realized from our SOA using cloud computing.

Second is the ability to change the IT infrastructure faster to adapt to the changing needs of the business, such as market downturns, or the introduction of a key product to capture a changing market. This, of course, provides a strategic advantage and gives the business a better chance of long-term survival. Many enterprises are plagued these days with having IT infrastructures that are so poorly planned and fragile that they hurt the business by not providing the required degree of agility.

Under the concept of reuse are a few things we must determine to better define the value:

- The number of services that are reusable
- Complexity of the services
- The degree of reuse from system to system

The number of reusable services is the actual number of new services created, or existing services abstracted, that are potentially reusable from system to system. The complexity of the services is the number of functions or object points that make up the service. We use traditional functions or object points as a common means of expressing complexity in terms of the types of behaviors the service offers. Finally, the degree of reuse from system to system is the number of times you actually reuse the services. We look at this number as a percentage.

Just because we abstract existing systems as services or create services from scratch, that does not mean that they have value until they are reused by another system. In order to determine their value, we must first determine the number of services that are available for reuse (NSR), the degree of reuse (DR) from system to system, and the complexity (C) of each service. The formula to determine value looks much like this:

Value = (NSR × DR) × C

Thus, if you have 100 services available for reuse (NSR = 100), the degree of reuse is 50% (DR = 0.50), and the complexity of each service is, on average, at 300 function points, the value would look like this:

Value = (100 × 0.5) × 300

or

Value = 15,000, in terms of reuse.

If you apply the same formula across domains, with consistent measurements of NSR, DR, and C, the relative value should be the resulting metrics. In other words, the amount of reuse directly translates into dollars saved. Also, keep in mind that we have to subtract the cost of implementing the services or creating the SOA using cloud computing, since that is the investment we made to obtain the value.

Moreover, the amount of money saved depends on your development costs, which vary greatly from company to company. Typically, you should know what you are paying for in function or object points, so it is just a matter of multiplication to determine the amount of money you are saving by implementing a particular SOA using cloud computing.

Agility is a strategic advantage that is difficult but not impossible to measure in hard dollars. We first need to determine a few things about the business:

- The degree of change over time
- The ability to adapt to change
- Relative value of change

The degree of change over time is really the number of times over a particular period that the business reinvents itself to adapt to a market. While a paper production company may have a degree of change of only 5% over a 5-year period, a high-technology company may have an 80% change over the same period.

The ability to adapt to change is a number that states the company's ability to react to the need for change over time. For instance, a larger computing manufacturer may need to change in order to drive into new markets but may not have a culture that can change at the rate required. It lacks the ability to adapt to change, so no matter what you do to accommodate change through the use of technology, such as SOA using cloud computing, the company will not be able to take advantage of it when considering the people issues.

Finally, the relative value of change is the amount of money made as a direct result of changing the business, such as a retail organization's ability to establish a frequent-buyer program to react to changing market expectations and the resulting increases in revenue from making that change.

These are just some basic guidelines around understanding and defining the value of agility and reuse as related to leveraging SOA using cloud computing.

Value of Leveraging Innovative Technology

Finally, we need to discuss the value of leveraging innovative, best-of-breed technology. This is important because the use of cloud computing could provide some less tangible benefits, such as the ability to raise more money and obtain more investors, since many view cloud computing as a more effective and efficient way to do IT. Thus, just using this technology may increase the value of the business, at least while people view cloud computing as a positive.

Putting a dollar amount on innovation is a bit difficult. However, it is the difference between what the market considers the value of the company when leveraging cloud computing versus a more traditional computing model. Of course, many organizations may leverage a bit of both, so you need to grade on a curve.

Making the Business Case

Instead of just giving you a bunch of high-level concepts that you may or may not consider helpful, it is a good exercise to actually walk you through the process of creating a business case for cloud computing. Keep in mind that you have a unique enterprise, so how you approach creating this business case is going to need some consideration of the business you are in, the size of your enterprise, and the people you work with. One size does not fit all, but there is enough information in the remainder of this chapter to get most business cases done.

The steps are

1. Understand the existing issues
2. Assign costs
3. Model "as is"
4. Model "to be"
5. Define value points
6. Define hard benefits
7. Define soft benefits
8. Create final business case

Step 1: Understand the Existing Issues

This is the big one. You need to list all of the existing business and IT issues. These are typically issues that hinder productivity or are major business processes that need attention. They should be detailed enough that you are defining a legitimate issue but not so detailed that you get lost in the minutia.

Moreover, you need to pick a domain. If yours is a Global 2000 company, then the enterprise is just too big; the problem domain needs to be a subset of systems that have the potential to become a project going forward—a project that should take less than a year to complete. So, keep your domains relevant but not too big. The sales automation system for an auto manufacturer would be an example of a good domain for creating a business case for cloud computing; the entire parts division of the auto manufacturer, consisting of 100 systems, would perhaps be too big.

Again, put them in business and IT buckets. For example, let's list issues for a sales automation domain. These are just examples, mind you:

Business
- Customer satisfaction is low due to lack of good sales automation processes.
- Sales projects are inaccurate, thus causing projected sales to be overstated and understated.

IT
- Existing hardware and software costs are not in alignment with best practices.
- Numerous system performance complaints are made by sales staff.
- Sales staff is forced to share terminals because of scaling limitations from the existing systems.

In essence, this is a list of business and IT issues we can potentially address with cloud computing. Again, the types of issues you use for your business case may be very different depending on the business and IT issues within your enterprises.

Step 2: Assign Costs

Now that we know the issues, we need to assign costs. These are typically going to be over a 1- or 2-year horizon, but some companies will want a 5-year horizon, depending on how they do the planning. This part of the business case is really about assigning cost to the defined issues, thus creating the case that there are things that can be improved, and here is how much we will benefit if we improve them.

Considering our example, we could assign yearly costs as follows:

Business

Customer satisfaction is low due to lack of good sales automation processes.	$500,000 in lost sales per year
Sales projections are inaccurate, thus causing projected sales to be overstated and understated.	$750,000 in the cost of poor reporting per year

IT

Existing hardware and software costs are not in alignment with best practices.	$1,000,000 in hardware/ software costs per year
Numerous system performance complaints are made by sales staff.	$200,000 in the cost of lost productivity per year
Sales staff is forced to share terminals because of scaling limitations from the existing systems.	$300,000 in the cost of lost productivity per year

Some of these costs are based on gathered data, others are estimated, and some are a mixture of both. Make sure that the cost of each issue is not inflated but is based on reality. Keep in mind that this business case will be reviewed at some time in the future and therefore should reflect the "real world" as much as possible.

Step 3: Model "As Is"

Modeling the "as is" means that we create a logical model of the current architecture within the domain, including all relevant systems, data, processes, services, and any other details that should be defined. Since this is really not an exercise in enterprise architecture, but an exercise in creating a business case, what is important about this step is that we have a clear understanding of the existing IT systems and what they do.

Step 4: Model "To Be"

Once we have modeled the as is, it's time to model the "to be." Again, this is not an architectural exercise—we talk about doing that during the remainder of the book—but you do need to define the to-be architecture so that the business case can be created. In other words, things are this bad (steps 1–3); we propose a solution that will make things better (step 4); and this is how much that solution will save us (steps 5–8).

This is where you propose the SOA using cloud computing solution if it is indeed needed, using the architectural guidelines provided in the remainder of the book—in essence, what the new architecture will look like, its components, its location, and so on. Consider that you are likely presenting this proposal to businesspeople, so too much talk about technology will not have the desired effect.

Step 5: Define Value Points

During this step, you define the value of the to-be architecture at a high level. For example, for many cloud computing solutions, the value points will be everything we presented at the beginning of this chapter, including

- Ongoing operational cost reduction
- The value of preserving capital
- The value of upsizing on demand
- The value of downsizing on demand
- The value of shifting the risk
- The value of agility
- The value of reuse
- The value of innovation

Step 6: Define Hard Benefits

In this step, we define the hard benefits in terms of direct and visible cost reduction and/or business efficiencies that are corrected. Refer to the list in step 5 as a jumping-off point to itemize and place dollar values next to the list of hard benefits, cost savings, or revenue-producing items that are easy to understand and quantify. The amount of money you place next to each benefit should have some detailed analysis around it.

For instance, when considering the value of preserving capital, you should use the analysis and concepts outlined earlier in this chapter. However, make sure to localize the analysis within your business to make the point: What does this hard benefit mean to your business? And list the numbers behind the hard benefits.

Step 7: Define Soft Benefits

Soft benefits are those value points that are difficult to quantify but are benefits nonetheless—for example, the value of better customer satisfaction (the value that customers see from better IT support of business processes they participate in) or the value of better employee moral (the value of being seen in your space as using modern technologies and thereby attracting or retaining better talent). We know the business benefits from these things, and here is where you attempt to quantify those benefits.

For instance, the use of as SOA using a cloud computing approach to provide better access to systems for key customers should result in X additional sales with Y margins and therefore Z profits. In many instances, the soft benefits are as valuable as, or more valuable than, the hard benefits when considering the business.

Step 8: Create the Final Business Case

Creating the business case is something we have been doing throughout this chapter, but here is where you write it down for the stakeholders. At a minimum, the business case should include

1. A clear understanding of the current business and IT issues the business is facing.
2. The amount of money these issues are costing the business.
3. The proposed improvements when leveraging SOA using cloud computing to address the identified business issues.

4. The amount of money, if any, that can be saved using these improvements.
5. Soft benefits.
6. Hard benefits.
7. Holistic impact on the business, good and bad.
8. Final proposed budget.
9. Suggestions for moving forward, or the ability for the SOA using cloud computing to benefit the business, or not.

It's All about the Business

While few will dispute the business value of SOA using cloud computing, there is always a need to create a business case that defines the value for a specific business. In most cases, you will find that cloud computing has a clear business value, but there are those cases where it does not, and thus it should not be used. You will not know until you define the business case and run the numbers.

One thing to keep in mind is that cloud computing is not free, and you have to consider the impact on IT holistically. Watch out for what is called the manage-by-magazine effect, where cloud computing is so much a part of popular thinking around computing that you are not objective. It is okay to say no to cloud computing if there is no clear business benefit. Also, cloud computing is clearly an architectural option for SOA. While you can do SOA without cloud computing, you cannot do cloud computing without SOA. Keep that in mind.

What is going to be difficult is creating business cases as the world of cloud computing continues to emerge. Simply put, we just do not know enough about cloud computing's long-term operational value or many of the pitfalls that may arise, since most of the public cloud computing providers that we are likely to leverage have not been around for all that long. You always need to consider this as a learning process, and make sure to look at the current state-of-the-art while leveraging the guidelines we put forth in this book. The technology will constantly change. The architecture should be relatively stable.

On the upside, we have a clear opportunity to change the way we do IT to have a more positive influence on the business when leveraging an SOA using cloud computing. No longer will IT be a drain on company resources, and many enterprises will find that the newfound efficiencies of IT have a huge value on the bottom line. After all, IT is there to serve business, and not the other way around.

At the close of this chapter, we assume that the business case is there for a SOA using cloud computing. Now we go forward with an understanding of the existing problem domain and move from the data to the services to the processes.

CHAPTER 5

Working from Your Data to the Clouds

*You can use all the quantitative data you can get,
but you still have to distrust it and use your
own intelligence and judgment.*

—Alvin Toffler

Let's step back a bit and look at what we are going to do here. In the next several chapters, I'll present a rudimentary methodology that extends your enterprise architecture out to the clouds. The basic steps of this methodology include the following:

1. Define the data.
2. Define the services.
3. Define the processes.
4. Define governance.
5. Define which candidate data, services, and processes should live in the clouds and which should live on-premise.

Let's say we did a wonderful job in creating a business case for cloud computing, as defined in Chapter 4, "Making the Business Case for Clouds," and now it is time to get to work. We start with what is easiest to define, the information, and work up from there.

The idea is that the better understanding we have around our existing information, service, and process models, the better chance that our move to the clouds will be successful. In some instances, the information presented in these next few chapters is based on existing approaches to defining and designing information technology that are well covered in many other books.

So, keep in mind as we go through this process that we are not interested in reinventing the wheel. Where existing IT concepts will work just fine, there is no need to change them. Indeed, the information presented here is applicable when considering other types of information systems as well.

You may recognize concepts that have been part of IT for years, including logical and physical database design, data dictionaries, and metadata. However, there are some new approaches that work especially well with SOA using cloud computing, including the use of ontologies and a common information model that spans a domain made up of many systems. In other words, create a common database that spans multiple on-premise and cloud computing systems but is logically the same and could be physically distributed in any number of ways, through on-premise or cloud computing.

Old or New?

Another issue we have to deal with in this chapter and the next few that cover services and processes is this: *Are we looking to relocate an existing system from on-premise to cloud computing, or are we defining a new system or systems that will reside in the clouds?*

For the most part, the next few chapters are about analysis of existing information systems (legacy systems). In most cases, we are looking at existing resources and coming to a deeper level of understanding before considering moving them to the clouds. Generally speaking, this is the most common use of cloud computing: the relocation of core on-premise information systems to cloud-based platforms to save some money or for other strategic reasons that we defined in Chapter 4.

However, in some cases, the systems will be new. There is really no overall change to the process other than that you do not have to start with existing information because you will be defining the data, services, and processes from scratch. However, you still need to apply all of the concepts in this chapter and the next few, including how to leverage ontologies, define the data, create core artifacts such as data dictionaries and data catalogs, and build the core information model, which is the core deliverable out of this part of the approach, as defined within this chapter.

The advantage of creating new systems in clouds is that you have a green field opportunity because you can define everything and you are not limited by an existing system that has predefined processes and data. The process of defining a new system should be much easier and much more fun. New start-ups today that leverage cloud computing have the ability to both design the systems for cloud computing platforms and leverage cloud computing out of the gate, which provides them with a key strategic advantage. You may assume that many startups that break out over the next few years will do so largely because their core IT operations costs are very low due to cloud computing. They will have more agility with those architectures as well.

Let's Get Some Context

This and the next two chapters—focused on understanding your data, services, and processes—are really about defining what you already have so that you have a complete understanding of what to place on a cloud computing platform within the context of a larger architecture. Those who just toss applications out onto clouds without this type of deep analysis will find that the end of the process is more difficult and time-consuming than if they had worked from a well-laid plan. This is true not just for a cloud computing architecture, but for any architecture, including those that use SOA approaches, which is really the purpose of this book: cloud computing and SOA convergence, or SOA using cloud computing.

Understanding the data, the topic of this chapter, requires defining all relevant metadata within the candidate applications, new or old, that you wish to place on cloud computing platforms. This means defining where the data is now, the data structure, the logical model, the physical model, security issues, data definitions, and so on. At the end of this process, you should have a populated metadata layer and a common information model (described later).

Understanding the services, the topic of Chapter 6, "Working from Your Services to the Clouds," means that we are looking at Web services, transactions, or APIs that are externalized by the existing candidate systems. The purpose of this process is to list them, understand them in detail, document them, and link them back to the information model we defined in the previous step. Again, we are attempting to understand existing or new services that either will

continued

be placed on a cloud computing platform or will interact with resources hosted in the clouds. Services provide a more granular way to deal with applications, because you can mix and match services that exist within the enterprise and on cloud computing resources, all bound together using processes (discussed next).

You need to understand all business processes, the topic of Chapter 7, "Working from Your Processes to the Clouds," that exist within your domain, either automated or not. This understanding is important because now that we know which services and information sources are available, we must define higher-level mechanisms for interaction, including all high-level, mid-level, and low-level processes. In many instances, these processes have yet to become automated or are only partially automated.

Data First

Let's start with the data and work up from there. There are several reasons to take a close look at the underlying information issues of our architecture before moving to cloud computing. First, you must have a good architectural foundation to move to SOA using cloud computing. You need to understand the underlying information no matter whether it is a new or an existing system. Again, some information is right for moving to an SOA using cloud computing platform, whereas in other instances it is contraindicated.

Second, moving from the data to the services to the processes and applications is a great way to move from the most primitive form of IT—simple information—to the most complex, from processes that have information and behavior to those with binding logic and sequence. In essence, we want to start small and simple, then move to large and complex.

You May Work in Any Direction

We advocate working from the data to the services and then to the processes. However, this rule is flexible. If it is a better fit, you could work from the processes to the services and then to the data.

> The reason we recommend working from the data is that information has a tendency to be the foundation for services, and processes are really just a logical grouping of services. However, the order is really up to you and the requirements of your problem domain.

Finally, we have found that looking closely at your current information issues is the best way to determine your information management needs before selecting the platform, on-premise or in the cloud. Define and understand the information before you select a platform.

You cannot deal with information you do not understand, and that includes information that will potentially exist in the cloud. Too often, people ignore the analysis of information and thus make huge mistakes regarding the proper use of information within services that may reside in the clouds. They ignore the application semantics (how an application defines data) and end up having to loop back and fix dysfunctional data structure, which costs a lot of money and a lot of time.

It is extremely important for you to identify all application semantics and metadata that exist in your domain, which will allow you to properly deal with that data within the context of your architecture, of how that data may reside on a cloud platform, and of your SOA in general.

The understanding of application semantics establishes the way and form in which a particular application refers to properties of the business process (see next Book Blog). For example, the very same customer number for one application may have a completely different value and meaning in another application. Understanding the semantics of an application guarantees that there will be no contradictory information when the new architecture is deployed, on-premise, in a cloud-based system, or in a combination.

Defining Data Concepts

Let's define some of the definitions that that are tossed about in this chapter.

Data: A collection of facts. Data is often viewed as a lowest level of abstraction from which information and knowledge are created.

continued

Information: A pattern of data that is meaningful, or data that is organized in a form that is meaningful.

Application semantics: The different ways in which data is represented within different applications. It is important here because, in many instances, we are looking at existing systems and thus a new way of dealing with the semantics of that system.

Metadata: Data about data. Enough said. We use it here as a common base of understanding as to how data is described, owned, secured, governed, and so on, by many different systems.

Ontologies: According to Wikipedia, "An ontology, in computer science and information science, is a formal representation of a set of concepts within a domain and the relationships between those concepts. It is used to reason about the properties of that domain, and may be used to define the domain."[1] We focus on the use of ontologies because of their ability to define relationships, which is just as important as defining the data.

Schema: The schema of a database system is its structure, supported by the database management system (DBMS). If you have a relational database, the schema is described as attributes or columns, tables, and rows, or a single piece of data. It is typically leveraged as part of the way of describing physical data derived from a logical database design.

Data dictionary: The *IBM Dictionary of Computing* defines data dictionary as a "centralized repository of information about data such as meaning, relationships to other data, origin, usage, and format."[2] This typically refers to a single system or application. The larger notion of a data dictionary is a data catalog (defined next), at least as we define the term in this book.

Data catalog: Data cataloging is about formalizing the information we gather, including the data dictionary. The difference is that the data dictionary is normally local to a single system or application, whereas the data catalog spans all systems in the problem domain.

Information model: It is best to think of the data catalog as the list of potential solutions to your architecture problem and to think of the information

---

1. http://en.wikipedia.org/wiki/Ontology_(information_science).
2. *IBM Dictionary of Computing*, 10th edition, ACM Press, 1993.

model as the architecture solution, or the "to be." Spanning the entire architecture, on-premise and cloud computing based, the information model is a master data model that depicts all major entities within the problem domain and how those entities are, or should be, related. In essence, it is an enterprise-common data model that is leveraged as a master point of reference for information as we build our architecture, or the target data layer definition we are implementing in our SOA using cloud computing. This is the deliverable out of this chapter, which is typically represented as logical and physical database models.

Selecting a Problem Domain

Before proceeding, you need to select a problem domain, or the area of the enterprise where you will be working. This is typically small, fewer than six systems. If you take on a huge area of the enterprise IT for this type of analysis, chances are that you will fail. It just gets too big and too complex. You need to select a working problem domain that is big enough to have an impact but small enough to complete the analysis within a reasonable amount of time. Use 2 to 3 months as a rule of thumb.

One of the most important things to keep in mind here is that we are looking at both new and existing systems for possible development or relocation onto cloud platforms as part of our SOA, or, in other words, extending our SOA to cloud computing platforms. As you select your problem domain, if there are organizational or political obstacles that will clearly prevent that movement in the future, solve those problems before doing this work.

Defining the Information Model

Once we select our problem domain, we can move into the core metadata analysis. Figure 5.1 depicts the proposed process for analyzing information that we use in the remainder of this chapter. We use similar processes in the next few chapters as well.

Defining the information model is a tough job because many of the existing systems you will deal with are older, proprietary, or perhaps both. In other instances, you will deal with systems yet to be built, but the same analysis

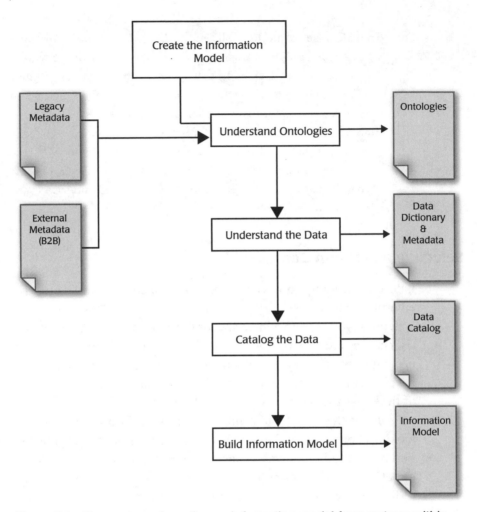

Figure 5.1   The process of creating an information model from systems within your problem domain.

must be completed. All architectures are unique in the way they define and store data.

Any technology that can reverse-engineer existing physical and logical database schemas will prove helpful in identifying structure and the basis of metadata within the problem domains. However, while the schema and database model may give insight into the structure of the database or databases, they cannot determine how that information is used within the context of the application or service; that is why we need the next several steps.

Understanding Ontologies

When dealing with SOA using cloud computing, as you know by now, we are dealing with much complexity. The notion of ontologies helps the enterprise and cloud computing architect prepare generalizations that make the problem domain more understandable. In contrast to abstraction, generalization ignores many of the details and ends up with general ideas (see Figure 5.2). Therefore, when generalizing, we start with a collection of types and analyze commonalities to generalize them. Figure 5.3 provides a good visual example of an ontology. Note how the nodes further define the general concepts.

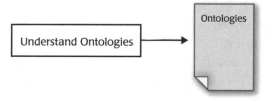

Figure 5.2   We use ontologies as a base for understanding. An ontology is used here to create a macro view of our problem domain, starting with the general concepts.

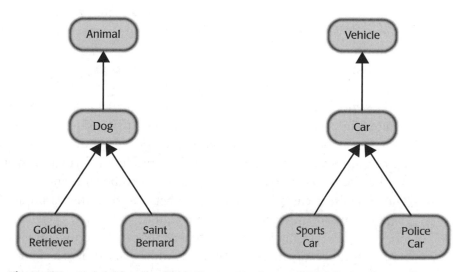

Figure 5.3   Ontologies provide better ways of organizing information and are a great tool for defining data as part of an SOA using cloud computing project.

You Can Skip Ontologies

While using ontologies is very helpful when dealing with complex problem domains with complex data, the use of ontologies as an approach to generalizing and understanding data within a problem domain is optional. Many architects delve right into the data analysis, skipping ontologies, and that is perfectly okay. We present ontologies here as an approach to analyzing data that can prove to be very productive.

Using ontologies as a starting point makes the more detailed analysis that much easier to deal with because we have already defined the general categories. From there, we can work down to the details of the metadata. We want to define the information within our problem domain more holistically before defining it in more detail. Ontological analysis clears the ground for generalization, making the properties of the entities much clearer. Ontological analysis for SOA using cloud computing encourages generalization.

One of the benefits of leveraging ontologies is that no matter where the information resides, we can understand and map information relevant to our SOA using cloud computing. Ontologies allow us to differentiate between resources, which is especially useful when those resources have redundant data (e.g., customer information in almost all enterprises). By making better sense of the data and representing the data in a meaningful way, terms defined in ontologies allow the architect to fully understand the meaning and context of the information.

An important notion of ontologies is entity correspondence. Ontologies that are leveraged in more of a distributed environment, such as business-to-business or cloud computing, must leverage data that is scattered across very different information systems and information that resides in many separate domains. Ontologies, in this scenario, provide a great deal of value because we can join information together, such as product information mapped to on-time delivery history, mapped to customer complaints and compliments. This establishes entity correspondence between data that is physically distributed, such as on-premise or within clouds.

To gather information specific to an entity, we need to leverage different resources to identify individual entities, which vary widely from each physical information store. For example, when leveraging a relational database, entities are identified using keys (e.g., customer numbers). Within the various information systems, many different terms are used for attributes. The notion of ontologies, in this scenario, allows us to determine whether entities from different applications and databases are the same or noncrucial to fusing information for the purposes of our data analysis.

Existing Web-Based Standards and Ontologies

The use of languages for ontology is beginning to appear, built on reasoning techniques that provide for the development of special-purpose reasoning services. In fact, the W3C created a Web standard for an ontology language as part of its effort to define semantic standards for the Web. The Semantic Web is the abstract representation of data on the World Wide Web based on the Resource Description Framework (RDF) and other standards still to be defined. It is being developed by the W3C in collaboration with a large number of researchers and industrial partners.

In order for the Semantic Web to function, computers must have access to structured collections of information and sets of inference rules that they can use to conduct automated reasoning. This notion is known as knowledge representation. To this end, and in the domain of the World Wide Web, computers will find the meaning of semantic data by following hyperlinks to definitions of key terms and rules for logical reasoning about data. The resulting infrastructure will spur the development of automated Web Services such as highly functional agents. What is important here is that the work now being driven by the W3C as a way to manage semantics on the Web is applicable, at least at the component level, to the world of application integration, much like XML and Web Services.

An example of the W3C contribution to the use of ontologies is the Web Ontology Language. OWL is a semantic markup language for publishing and sharing ontologies on the World Wide Web. OWL is derived from the DAML+OIL Web Ontology Language and builds on the RDF. OWL assigns a specific meaning to certain RDF triples. The future Formal Specification, now in development at the W3C, specifies exactly which triples are assigned a specific meaning and offers a definition of the meaning. OWL provides a semantic interpretation only for those parts of an RDF graph that instantiate the schema. Any additional RDF statements resulting in additional RDF triples are allowed, but OWL is silent on the semantic consequences of such additional

continued

triples. An OWL ontology is made up of several components, some of which are optional and some of which may be repeated.

Using these Web-based standards as the jumping-off point for ontology and cloud computing, it is possible to define and automate the use of ontologies in both intracompany and intercompany domains. Domains made up of thousands of systems, all with their own semantic meanings, are bound together in a common ontology that makes short work of cloud computing and defines a common semantic meaning of data in and between on-premise and cloud-based systems.

Extending from the languages, we have several libraries available for a variety of vertical domains, including financial services and e-business. We also have many knowledge editors that support the creation of ontologies, as well as the use of natural-language processing methodologies. We have seen these in commercially available knowledge mapping and visualization tools using standard notations such as Unified Modeling Language (UML).

Ontologies and Web standards that support ontologies are nothing new. However, considering that cloud computing provides a centralized location to create and share ontologies, I suspect it will become more important to architecture in general and to architecture that leverages cloud computing.

Understanding the Data

We know that if we look at cloud computing, we need to understand where the data exists, gather information about the data (e.g., schema and metadata information), and apply business principles to determine which data flows where and why (see Figure 5.4). This step fits into the larger steps that are depicted in Figure 5.5.

In short, implementing a cloud-based solution demands more than the movement and persistence of data within all systems in the problem domain. A successful solution requires that the enterprise also define how that information flows through it and how it is related to core services and core business processes (defined in Chapters 6 and 7).

In essence, what we are doing here is getting down to the details about the existing data, or data that is a part of new information systems. We are not analyzing this information as a component that will certainly reside in the clouds, but to provide a base of understanding to consider whether the information

Figure 5.4 Understanding the data is the most laborious part of the process. It means that we have to look at the specifics of the information/data and create traditional deliverables such as a data dictionary that defines the metadata. This is the most important step in this chapter.

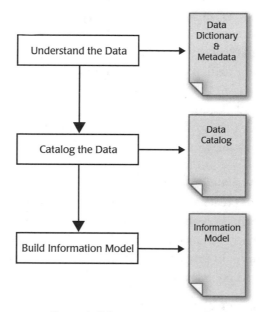

Figure 5.5 As we move through this process, we go from the systems-specific and/or application-specific data to a formal information model that spans the problem domain.

and the core systems could or should reside in the clouds and to have a good understanding of how to build those cloud-based systems if they do.

Identifying the Data

Unfortunately, there are no shortcuts to identifying data within an enterprise. All too often, information about the data—both business and technical—is scattered throughout the enterprise and is of a quality that ranges from "some-what useful" to "You've got to be kidding me!"

The first step in identifying and locating information about the data is to create a list of systems in the problem domain. This list makes it possible to determine which databases exist in support of those systems. The next step requires determining who owns the databases, where they are physically lo-cated, relevant design information, and such basic information as brand, model, and revisions of the database technology.

Any technology that can reverse-engineer existing physical and logical database schemas will prove helpful in identifying data within the problem domains. However, while the schema and database models may give insight into the structure of the database or databases, they cannot determine how that information is used within the context of the application. Moreover, in some instances, that data is part of a packaged information system, such as an enterprise resource planning (ERP) package or a customer relationship management (CRM) package, and you must rely on that packaged applica-tion vendor to provide the information around the data and sometimes ac-cess to the data.

Creating the Data Dictionary

You need to create a data dictionary as a base to hold all of the metadata and other information about the data you analyze. We do these per system be-cause in many instances, the systems are so different that it is difficult to find a common set of properties to track in the data dictionary. Information typi-cally tracked includes

- The reason for the existence of particular data elements
- Ownership
- Format
- Security parameters
- The role within both the logical and physical data structures

There are tools, such as repositories, that provide prebuilt systems for creating and maintaining a data dictionary, and some databases have data dictionaries built into the DBMS. Do not get caught up in how the data dic-tionary will be maintained—you can transfer it from tool to tool. For now, just focus on listing the correct information.

Understand Integrity Issues

When analyzing databases for cloud computing, integrity issues constantly crop up. In order to address these, it is important to understand the rules and logic that were applied to the construction of the database. For example, will the application allow the update of customer information in a customer table without first updating demographics information in the demographics table?

Most middleware, such as the middleware that connects on-premise systems to clouds, take into account the structure or rules built into the databases being connected. As a result, there exists the very real threat of damage to the integrity of target databases when relationships are not properly understood and/or defined.

While some databases, including on-premise and cloud-based systems, do come with built-in integrity controls (such as stored procedures or triggers), most rely on the application logic to handle integrity issues on behalf of the database. Unfortunately, the faith implicit in this reliance is not always well placed. All too often, it is painfully naïve when you consider that your cloud computing system will be widely distributed, which makes it difficult to create a common control mechanism to protect database integrity.

The lack of integrity controls at the data level (or, in the case of existing integrity controls, bypassing the application logic to access the database directly) could result in profound problems. Architects and developers must approach this danger cautiously, making sure they do not compromise databases' integrity in their zeal to move to cloud computing.

Understand Data Latency

Data latency, the characteristic of the data that defines how current the information needs to be, is another property of the data that must be determined for the purposes of leveraging cloud computing. Such information allows the architects to determine when the information should be copied or moved to another enterprise system, such as on-premise to the clouds, and how fast.

While an argument can be made to support a number of different categories of data latency, for our purpose of defining architecture for cloud computing, there are really only three:

1. Real-time
2. Near-time
3. Some-time

Real-time data is precisely what it sounds like: information that is placed in the database as it occurs, with little or no latency. Monitoring stock price information through a real-time feed from Wall Street is an example of real-time data. Real-time data is updated as it enters the database, and that information is available immediately to anyone or to any application requiring it for processing.

While zero-latency real time is clearly the goal, achieving it represents a huge challenge. In order to achieve something near zero latency, cloud computing implementation requires constant returns to the database, application, or other resource to retrieve new and/or updated information. In the context of real-time updates, database performance must also be considered; simultaneous to one process updating the database as quickly as possible, another process must be extracting the updated information.

Near-time data is information that is updated at set intervals rather than instantaneously. Stock quotes posted on the Web are a good example of near-time data. They are typically delayed 20 minutes or more, since the Web sites distributing the quotes are generally unable to process real-time data. Near-time data can be thought of as "good-enough" latency data—in other words, data only as timely as needed.

Although near-time data is not updated constantly, providing it still presents many of the same challenges as real-time data, including overcoming performance and management issues.

Some-time data is typically updated only once within a given time period. Customer addresses or account numbers are examples of some-time information. Within the context of an SOA using cloud computing architecture, the intervals of data copy or data movement do not require the kind of aggressiveness needed to accomplish real-time or near-time data exchange.

The notion of data typing goes well beyond the classification of the data as real-time, near-time, or some-time. It is really a complex process of determining the properties of the data, including updates and edit increments, as well as the behavior of the data over time. What do the applications use the particular data for? How often do they use it? What happens with the data over time? These questions must be addressed in order to create the most effective SOA using a cloud computing solution. Here is where you do that.

CASE STUDY: DEFINING THE DATA FOR BLUE MOUNTAIN HAMMOCKS

Let's use a mini case study to make the concepts and processes presented in this chapter a bit clearer. We continue to use this case study in the next two chapters to demonstrate how we move from the data to the services to the processes so that we can understand our problem domain and perhaps take advantage of cloud computing using SOA approaches and best practices.

Blue Mountain Hammocks, or BMH, was founded in 1973 and has more traditional IT in place, including

- A sales automation system that uses Oracle as the database, with the application built in C++. This application is also connected to BMH's online store.
- An open source inventory management system built using Java and MySQL.
- A general ledger system that uses a packaged accounting system built using dBase, a PC-based database.

They all run on different hardware and software platforms, on-premise.

The BMH management team wants to save some IT costs and believe cloud computing could be a potential solution. The team is aware that BMH's existing IT operations cannot expand quickly enough to keep up with the company's growth rate. Also, the existing architecture cannot quickly adjust to changes in the business, including moving into new product lines such as manufacturing and selling lawn furniture, which requires very different business processes. The company needs the ability to expand quickly, on demand, and the ability to change processes, as needed, in support of any beneficial directions of the business.

Let's look at aspects of BMH's data for the purposes of this chapter. In a very simplified form, the core data is as follows.

Sales Automation Database
Customer
    CustNum (char 20)
    Fname (char 10)
    Lname (char 15)
    CompanyName (char 15)
    Address (char 30)
    City (char 20)
    Zip (char 5)

Sales
    CustNum (char 20)
    Date (date)
    SaleAmount (num 20)
    ProductSold (char 10)

Inventory Management Database
Products
    ProductID (char 10)
    ProductDesc (char 40)
    ProductWeight (num 10)
    AmountOnHand (num 10)

General Ledger Database
Customers
    CNum (char 30)
    CName (char 30)
    CAddress (char 40)
    CCity (char 30)
    CZip (char 5)
Products
    PNum (char 30)
    PDesc (char 40)
    PPrice (num 10)
Sales
    CNum (char 30)
    PNum (char 30)
    SAmount (num 10)

We need to create a data dictionary, if not currently in place, for each system. Then, we create a domainwide data catalog. Finally, we create the information model.

The data dictionaries are pretty simple for this problem domain because the data is well defined in each database. It is just a matter of adding a description and some other information, including

- The reason for the existence of particular data elements
- Ownership
- Format
- Security parameters
- The role within both the logical and physical data structures

There is not a set format or rules around what a data dictionary should consist of. A quick and dirty listing of the data is just fine. We just need to provide a base understanding of all the existing data to move to the next step in cataloging the data.

The data catalog for this problem domain is the combination of all the data dictionaries into one common place, using one common approach and format. This the first step in abstracting the data structures from their physical instances into a common listing of data assets that we will use to determine our "to-be" database solution, including any use of cloud computing resources that may a fit once we are through this process. The data catalog (very much simplified) for our BMH problem domain may look like Table 5.1.

This is just a raw listing of the data elements found in all of the data dictionaries, in this case three. However, you need to add some additional information, including

- Description
- Ownership
- Security parameters
- Integrity parameters
- Dependencies

Again, there are no set rules for what should be contained in a data catalog, so you can create a data catalog that best meets your requirements.

Moving on to the information model, it is a good idea to identify the common entities in this problem domain. In our BMH example, we have

1. Customer
2. Sales
3. Products

That simple. It is also good to define the relationships, such as *Customer buys Products, which creates Sales.*

Again, not complex.

So, the to-be or target information model that we consider when building our SOA using cloud computing could be as follows:

Customer
    Customer_Number
    Customer_Name
    Company_Name
    Customer_Address
    Customer_State
    Customer_Zip

Table 5.1   Blue Mountain Hammocks Data Catalog

Name	System	Owner	Format	Description
CustNum	SA		(char 20)	
Fname	SA		(char 10)	
Lname	SA		(char 15)	
CompanyName	SA		(char 15)	
Address	SA		(char 30)	
City	SA		(char 20)	
Zip	SA		(char 5)	
CustNum	Inventory		(char 20)	
Date	Inventory		(date)	
SaleAmount	Inventory		(num 20)	
ProductSold	Inventory		(char 10)	
ProductID	Inventory		(char 10)	
ProductDesc	Inventory		(char 40)	
ProductWeight	Inventory		(num 10)	
AmountOnHand	Inventory		(num 10)	
CNum	GL		(char 30)	
CName	GL		(char 30)	
CAddress	GL		(char 40)	
CCity	GL		(char 30)	
CZip	GL		(char 5)	
PNum	GL		(char 30)	
PDesc	GL		(char 40)	
PPrice	GL		(num 10)	
CNum	GL		(char 30)	
PNum	GL		(char 30)	
SAmount	GL		(num 10)	

Product
    Product_Number
    Product_Description
    Product_Size
    Product_Weight
    Product_Price
Sales
    Customer_Number
    Product_Number
    Amount_Sold
    Date_Sold

Again, it's very simple to make our point here. Clearly, your problem domain will deal with many more data elements, entities, and complexities, but the core idea is the same.

The resulting information model, or the final outcome of this process, is less complex and is easy to understand, but it also represents all of the information as discovered in our current systems, including groupings of data around Customer, Product, and Sales.

The idea is to move from the complex and ill defined to the logical and well defined, thus having a complete understanding of the as-is and to-be states of your data level before moving on to services and processes, covered next.

Data Cataloging

Data cataloging is about formalizing the information we gather in the previous two steps (see Figure 5.6), including the data dictionary. The difference is that the data dictionary is typically local to a single system or application, whereas the data catalog spans all systems in the problem domain.

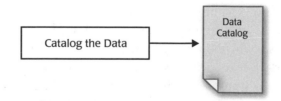

Figure 5.6 Before building the information model, we need to catalog all of the data previously defined in the data dictionary. We do this to make it easier to break out the data as we look to relocate some systems to the clouds.

A good data catalog should list all data elements within all systems, making sure to record

- Description
- Ownership
- System
- Format
- Security parameters
- Integrity parameters
- Dependencies

Once accomplished, it is possible to create an enterprisewide and/or cloudwide catalog of all data elements that may exist within the enterprise or on the cloud computing platforms. The resulting catalog becomes the basis of understanding that is needed to create the core information model—the foundation of our architecture and the basis for figuring out what will exist in the clouds and what will not.

For most medium- to large-sized enterprises, the creation of this data catalog is a massive undertaking. In essence, it demands the creation of the Mother of All Data Dictionaries, a complex directory that includes not only the traditional data dictionary information but also all of the information that is of interest to a cloud project, such as system information, security information, ownership, connected processes, communications mechanisms, and integrity issues, along with such traditional metadata as format, name of attribute, description, and so on.

While there is no standard for cataloging data within cloud computing projects, or any architecture project for that matter, the guiding principle stands clear: the more information, the better. The catalog will become both the repository for the new architecture to be built and the foundation to discover new business flows. It will also become a way to automate existing business flows within the enterprise.

It is an understatement to suggest that this catalog will be huge. Most enterprises will find tens of thousands of data elements to identify and catalog even while reducing redundancies among some of the data elements. In addition to being huge, the data catalog will be a dynamic structure. In a very real sense, it will never be complete. A person, or persons, will have to be assigned to maintain the data catalog over time, assuring that the information in the catalog remains correct and timely and that the architects and developers have access to the catalog in order to create the SOA using cloud computing.

Building the Information Model

Once all the information about all the data in the enterprise is contained in the data catalog, it is time to focus on the enterprise metadata model, or what we call the information model. The difference between the two is sometimes subtle. It is best to think of the data catalog as the list of potential solutions to your architecture problem and to think of the information model as the final data architecture solution (see Figure 5.7).

Let's review:

- *Data dictionary:* What data exists currently, per system and/or application, and the definitions of that data (metadata)
- *Data catalog:* Domainwide, sometimes enterprisewide, data dictionary
- *Information model:* The final to-be state of the data architecture for our SOA using cloud computing and the jumping-off point for figuring out which data should reside on cloud computing platforms and which should reside on-premise

The metadata model defines all of the data structures that exist in the enterprise as well as how those data structures will interact within the architecture solution domain. While you can express your information model in any number of ways, it is usually best to create a logical model and a physical model. Keep in mind that we do not know the target platforms as of yet, so the models should be technology and platform independent at this point.

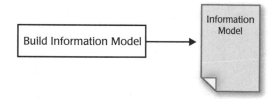

Figure 5.7 The final step is to complete the information model. This is the reference model used to define the final data architecture that provides us with a jumping-off point to figure out the data that should remain on-premise or reside on cloud computing platforms.

Logical Model

Just as with traditional database design methods, the enterprise metadata model used for information-level architecture can be broken into two components: the logical and the physical. And, just as with the former, the same techniques apply to the latter. Creating the logical model is the process of creating an architecture for all data stores that are independent of a physical database model, development tool, or a particular DBMS (e.g., Oracle, Sybase, Informix).

A logical model is a sound approach to an architecture project in that it allows architects and developers the opportunity to make objective information-level architecture decisions, moving from high-level requirements to implementation details. The logical data model is an integrated view of business data throughout the application domain or data pertinent to the architecture solution under construction, typically represented as an ERD, or entity relationship diagram (see Figure 5.8). The primary difference between using a

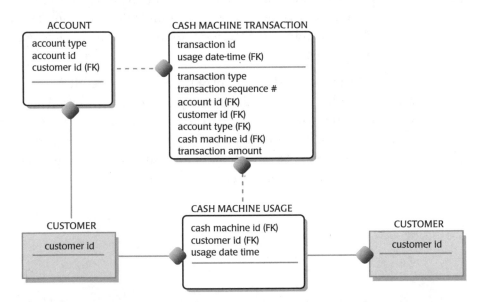

Figure 5.8 The logical data model is usually represented as an entity relationship diagram. This ERD is fully attributed, meaning the entities are defined along with the data structures. (From Linthicum, *Enterprise Application Integration*, Figure 6.3 p. 102, © 2000 by Addison-Wesley. Reproduced by permission of Pearson Education, Inc.)

logical data model for architecture versus traditional database development is the information source. While traditional development, generally speaking, defines new databases based on business requirements, a logical data model arising from an architecture project is based on existing databases.

Physical Model

The myriad of database types in any given enterprise minimizes the importance of the physical enterprise model because with so many database types, the physical model will rarely be used. The reason is clear: there is simply no clear way to create a physical model that maps down to object-oriented, multidimensional, hierarchy, flat files, and relational databases all at the same time. However, if those databases are to be integrated, some common physical representation must be selected. Only then can the model be transformed as required.

Our discussion of the physical model is only for those times when it is possible to map the logical to the physical—that is, when an enterprise uses a homogeneous database approach, usually all relational. The input for the physical model is both the logical model and the data catalog. When accessing this information, consider the data dictionary, business rules, and other user processing requirements.

Importance of Data with SOA Using Cloud Computing

We begin with the data because it is the foundation for most information systems and a good way to define what these systems do before we potentially relocate them to the clouds. However, the concepts and activities presented in this chapter are not at all new; they map back to core architectural activities, including SOA. The purpose here is to understand the existing state of the data, define the data at a detailed level, and then define the final to-be data architecture that allows us to figure out which data should physically reside on-premise or on cloud computing platforms. However, this is all about doing SOA with the new architectural options of cloud computing.

What is new is that, for our target architecture, some of the information systems will not be under our direct control. However, not much more than that changes. We still need to define how the data is structured, as well as relationships between the data, integrity, security, and all things in between. The big difference is that eventually we need to figure out how to manage data be-tween on-premise and cloud-based systems, making sure that they function as if they exist within the same data center. That should be the objective.

Many times when moving to new concepts such as cloud computing, ar-chitects and application designers have a tendency to neglect the fundamentals of the architecture, including the data. You do this at the risk of architecture failure and the failure of any instances of cloud-based systems you build from that architecture. Those who do not grasp the underlying data will not be able to define the information systems that they will need, clouds or no clouds.

CHAPTER 6

Working from Your Services to the Clouds

Doing nothing is very hard to do . . . you never know when you're finished.

—Leslie Nielsen

What is a service, and why do we care? Services denote behavior, or what is done by a service, such as

- Update customer
- Delete customer
- Calculate insurance risk
- Do a credit check

Services are not specific to cloud computing or to SOA, for that matter. They are a way to describe how we can access specific behaviors and data. Services are typically exposed out of an application and provide a way to access the value of the application, both behavior and data, using a well-defined interface.

We can think of services as collections of functional behaviors, each callable individually or as a group. You can mix and match services to form composite applications, or you can combine many services into a single composite application. This approach provides flexibility for the architecture, including the ability to leverage cloud computing resources and the ability to change the architecture as needed by the business.

In the case of cloud computing, this means the ability to run applications and their services, on-premise or within the clouds, and have those services available to any application, on-premise or in the clouds. This is an important step in looking at candidate applications and services that may make sense to move to cloud computing platforms. The idea is to address them as services and make them platform and location independent. Can you invoke them from any platform, cloud-based or on-premise? That is the goal: defined services that may exist on cloud-based or on-premise systems and are accessible from both systems.

To make this a bit easier to understand, let's walk through this process. Figure 6.1 depicts the beginning state of the architecture, typically with all services and systems hosted on-premise and nothing yet in the cloud or clouds. Each system has a set of services that it can expose (represented by the circles), thereby providing interfaces to other applications by using services—the basic idea behind a SOA.

The purpose of this chapter is to introduce the concept of services and explain how to leverage them as an effective way to approach cloud comput-

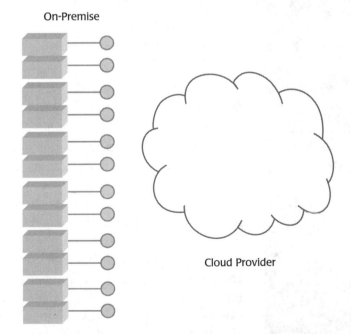

Figure 6.1   The "Before." As we begin to relocate systems to the cloud, we must first gain a service-level understanding, which is what we define in this chapter.

ing. If you think this sounds like SOA, in many ways it is. However, as we discussed in Chapter 1, "Where We Are, How We Got Here, and How to Fix It,"
and as demonstrated in this chapter, SOA approaches are the correct on-
ramp to cloud computing, with cloud computing providing architectural
options for the architecture. Thus, at a high level, the process is as follows:

1. Understand the existing as-is architecture.
2. Identify the existing services within the architecture.
3. Document and list those services within a directory.
4. Define the to-be architecture, including the use of cloud computing.

As depicted in Figure 6.2, once we have a service-level understanding of
the problem domain, we can identify systems and services that are good candidates for relocation into cloud platforms and those that can stay on-premise.
(We get into how that relocation occurs in subsequent chapters.) The idea is
that we will relocate the systems to find a more cost-effective way to process the

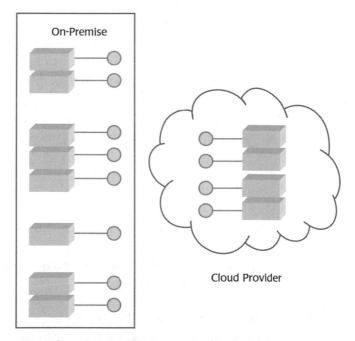

Figure 6.2   The "After." Once we have a service-level understanding of the problem
domain, we can begin to relocate systems to the cloud-based platforms where it
makes sense. Keep in mind that the systems can still communicate using services.

same applications and services but never give up the ability to leverage these systems and services. Services are typically location and platform independent. This means that no matter where the services exist, on-premise or cloud-based, they are accessible as if they were local.

In many architectural systems, we would create new services as part of the services model. This book looks at methods to extend an SOA to cloud computing if that approach make sense. Thus, we limit our discussion to identifying existing services, documenting those services, and relocating those services if cost justified. Keep in mind that you could be building new services as part of this process.

Again, the ability to address all of these systems through services provides the architect with the ability to access the underlying application behavior and information as if the application and services were native and local. The use of services provides location independence, meaning you can leverage services no matter where they exist. A single application could be made up of dozens of services hosted in a dozen different locations, on-premise and in the clouds. This is why we use services within the context of a widely distributed system, including an SOA using cloud computing.

Since they all expose information and behaviors as services, which typically use a common and standard interface such as Web Services, they are location independent (cloud or on-premise), platform independent, programming language independent, and user interface independent—that is, if they are properly created.

Continuing with our case study from Chapter 5, "Working from Your Data to the Clouds," Blue Mountain Hammocks, or BMH, has

- A sales automation system that uses Oracle as the database, with the application built in C++. This application is also connected to BMH's online store.
- An open source inventory management system built using Java and MySQL.
- A general ledger system that uses a packaged accounting system built using dBase, a PC-based database.

They all run on different hardware and software platforms, on-premise.

BMH wants to understand its architecture and potentially move pieces of it to cloud computing. We already obtained a data-level understanding when we created the information model in Chapter 5.

Using a simplistic approach that allows us to cover this problem domain/ architecture in a single chapter, let's say that we found the following candidate services within the following systems:

Sales Automation
    Add_Customer
    Del_Customer
    Edit_Customer
    Add_Sales
    Del_Sales
    Edit_Sale
    Perform_Credit_Check

Inventory Management
    Add_Product
    Del_Product
    Edit_Product
    Order_Product

General Ledger
    Add_Customer
    Del_Customer
    Update_Customer
    Add_Account
    Update_Account
    Add_Product
    Del_Product
    Update_Product
    Record_Sales
    Update_Sales

The use of this SOA to leveraging cloud computing provides us with a few key advantages:

- We have the ability to leverage services from anywhere, as required by the architecture in support of the business. For example, we can leverage a credit check service hosted on a cloud-based platform from any systems within the architecture, on-premise or cloud-based. Since you deal with applications at the services level, they are location and platform independent, and it should not matter where they are hosted.
- We have the ability to leverage virtualization, or address core applications as logical instances that may run on any number of physical server

instances, providing better resource utilization and scalability. In essence, you talk to the applications through the services interface. The location where the instance actually runs is transparent to you.

▪ We have the ability to mix and match services for use within composite applications or composite processes. This provides the agility aspect with the use of cloud computing architecture and SOA. Not only can you create application processes quickly to solve business problems, but you can recreate them as needed and thus provide the core value of agility. The use of cloud computing provides even more value because we do this using more cost-effective computing platforms.

Thus, we have the purpose of this chapter: the need to deal with all of our IT assets as services. We must define them with enough detail to figure out how they work and play well within our SOA and how some of those services may reside on cloud platforms if we need them to live there. Assuming that you are an enterprise or SOA architect, we provide you with enough information about the "how" that you can be productive in your own cloud computing replatform project.

Before we continue with our case study, let's get back to the basics.

Services Provide the Moving Parts

We look at our architecture as a collection of services, and thus as an SOA, because it is much easier to break the architecture down to a logical, functional primitive and build it back up as a defined set of services. Once we do that, we have a starting point for figuring out which services should exist on-premise and which services should potentially reside in the cloud (see Figures 6.1 and 6.2).

We build services on top of data or information, which we defined in the previous chapter as the information model. We did that first because services typically process information or are bound to data. In many instances, it is much easier to define services after defining data, but some choose to do the reverse, from the services to the data. Either way works, and how you approach this depends on your problem domain and on your own requirements and preferences.

At this point, you have a data-level understanding of your problem domain, and now we move up to a service-level understanding (see Figure 6.3).

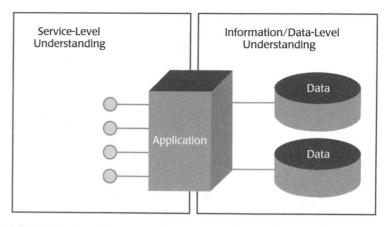

Figure 6.3 In Chapter 5, we created an information model, or a data/information-level understanding. In this chapter, we look at application behaviors that may be exposed, or a service-level understanding.

Figure 6.4 shows us the process we follow in this chapter, moving from a data-level understanding where we created the information model of the problem domain to a service-level understanding. Thus, we have the core service model, which provides a jumping-off point to cloud computing, or at least a foundation to make core architecture calls around the processing of services, either on-premise or in the cloud.

The *candidate services* are all services identified within the problem domain that have the potential of becoming services. We list them to make sure we identify the right services by identifying and sorting through *all* services. This deliverable is nothing more than a list of services and what each does.

We defined the candidate services for our case study earlier in this chapter, creating a basic list of the services that we think should be services, but we are not sure yet. The rule of thumb is, when in doubt, add it in as a candidate service. You can always remove it later.

Services and information creates the links between the candidate services and the data that is bound to the services. For instance, when considering the Update_Customer service, we can determine that Update_Customer is bound to customer data, perhaps First_Name, Last_Name, and Customer_Number. We talk more about this in the next section. However, let's look at this in the context of our case study.

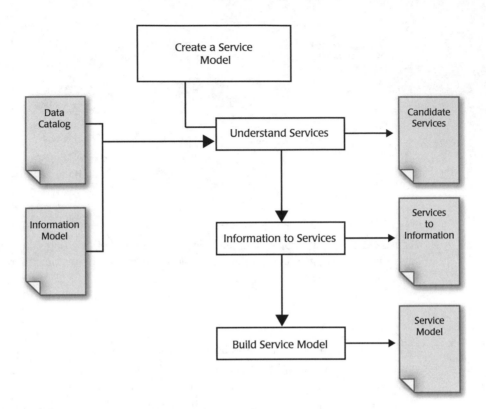

Figure 6.4   Creating the service model requires an understanding of the information, including the data catalog and the information model we created in Chapter 5. Key deliverables include candidate services, services as related to information, and the service model.

Looking only at the General Ledger system, we discovered the following information when we created the information model:

General Ledger Database
Customers
    CNum (char 30)
    CName (char 30)
    CAddress (char 40)
    CCity (char 30)
    CZip (char 5)

Products
    PNum (char 30)
    PDesc (char 40)
    PPrice (num 10)

Sales
    CNum (char 30)
    PNum (char 30)
    SAmount (num 10)

And we have the following candidate services:

    Add_Customer
    Del_Customer
    Update_Customer
    Add_Account
    Update_Account
    Add_Product
    Del_Product
    Update_Product
    Record_Sales
    Update_Sales

Looking at just the services that touch the customer table, we can say that

    Add_Customer
    Del_Customer
    Update_Customer

are bound to:

    Customers
    CNum (char 30)
    CName (char 30)
    CAddress (char 40)
    CCity (char 30)
    CZip (char 5)

We have identified services and linked them to an operational database. Now we have the information and the behavior that acts on that information.

Finally, the *service model* is the listing of all services from the candidate services list that are relevant and thus selected as services for our architecture. Moreover, they are decomposed and ordered so all services dependent on other services are understood, from the highest level to the lowest. For instance, the service Rent a Car is made up of Reserve a Car, Pick Up Car, Drop off Car. However, the service Reserve a Car is made up of Identify Customer, Select Car, and Enter Reservation. You get the idea. In essence, we define the services as they exist in a hierarchy, from the highest to the lowest level, not forgetting to define the data that is bound to those services.

For instance, let's go back to our candidate services for General Ledger: Update_Product may be decomposed to:

1. Update_Product
   1.1 Add_Product
   1.2. Edit_Product
   1.3. Del_Product
   1.4. Check_Product

While decomposing services should be considered an architectural exercise, this process can be done by anybody who is looking at cloud computing as an architectural option, including developers and project leaders. It is really some quick analysis to determine a basis of understanding to look at cloud computing options, not a complete and rigorous architectural process as defined by some SOA and enterprise architecture approaches and methodologies.

Now that we know what we are looking for—basic concepts, the general process, and how to proceed—let's spend the remainder of the chapter getting into some useful details.

What Is a Service?

Good question. Here is a better question: *What is a service, and how does it differ from information we discussed in Chapter 5?* When using a service, we leverage a remote method or behavior rather than simply extract or publish information to a remote system. We typically abstract this remote service into another application, known as a composite application, which is usually made up of more than one service.

A good example of a service is a risk analysis process, which runs within an enterprise to calculate the risk of a financial transaction. This remote application service is of little use by itself, but when abstracted into a larger application—for example, a trading system—that remote application service has additional value.

Note that we leverage the behavior of this remote service more than the information it produces or consumes. If you are a programmer, you can view application services as subroutines or methods—something you invoke to make something happen.

The basic notion of SOA and SOA using cloud computing is to leverage these remote services using some controlled infrastructure that allows applications to invoke remote application services as if they were local to the application. The result (or goal) is a composite application made up of many local and remote application services. Since they are location and platform independent, they can reside on-premise or within one of many cloud computing providers.

Furthermore, once services are identified and exposed or are developed from scratch, we may have services that span both on-premise and cloud-enabled platforms (see Figure 6.5). In essence, once the services are identified

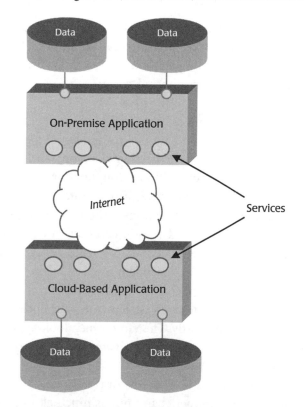

Figure 6.5 Services exist in both on-premise and cloud-based applications and can be invoked on either platform using a standard service interface, such as Web Services.

and exposed, we can place them on on-premise or cloud-delivered platforms, as depicted earlier in Figures 6.1 and 6.2.

Keep in mind that services have the following capabilities within this type of architecture:

- The ability to invoke services as if they were native no matter where they exist, on-premise or cloud-based, over the local network or the Internet.
- The ability to mix and match services within composite applications or processes, since the interfaces are typically standard (e.g., Web Services Description Language and Simple Object Access Protocol).
- The ability to manage and govern services centrally.

Understanding Coupling for the Clouds

One of the key concepts to consider when talking about services and cloud computing is the notion of coupling. We need to focus on this because in many instances, coupling is not a good architectural choice considering that the services are not only hosted within separate data centers but hosted by one or more cloud computing providers.

Since the beginning of computing, we have been dealing with the notion of coupling, or the degree that one component is dependent on another component, in the domains of both applications and architectures. Lately, the movement has been toward loose coupling for some very good reasons, but many architects who build enterprise architectures that leverage cloud computing understand the motivations behind this because we do not want to become operationally dependent on a component we do not own nor control.

Breaking this concept down to its essence, we can state that tightly coupled systems/architectures are dependent on each other. Thus, changes to any one component may prompt changes to many other components. Loosely coupled systems/architectures, in contrast, leverage independent components and thus can operate independently. Therefore, when looking to create an SOA and leverage cloud computing resources, generally speaking, the best approach is a loosely coupled architecture.

Keep in mind that how loosely or tightly coupled your architecture exists is a matter of requirements and not as much about what is popular. Architects must understand the value of cloud computing and loose coupling and make the right calls to insure that the architecture matches the business objectives. It is helpful to walk through this notion of coupling as you approach your cloud computing architecture.

With the advent of Web Services and SOA, we have been seeking to create architectures and systems that are more loosely coupled. Loosely coupled systems provide many advantages, including support for late or dynamic binding to other components while running and can mediate the difference in the component's structure, security model, protocols, and semantics, thus abstracting volatility.

This is in contrast to compile time or late binding, which requires that you bind the components at compile time or runtime (synchronous calls), respectively, and also requires that changes be designed into all components at the same time because of the dependencies. As you can imagine, this type of coupling is almost unheard of when leveraging cloud computing platforms for processes that span on-premise to the cloud providers because the systems need to function independently.

The advantages of loosely coupled architectures, as found within many SOAs and should be leveraged with SOA using cloud computing, are apparent to many of us who have built architectures and systems in the past, at least from a technical perspective. However, they have business value as well.

First and foremost, a loosely coupled architecture allows you to replace or change components without having to make reflective changes to other components in the architecture/systems. This means businesses can change their business systems as needed with much more agility than if the architecture/systems were more tightly coupled.

Second, developers can pick and choose the right enabling technology for the job without having to concern themselves with technical dependencies such as security models. Thus, you can build new components using a cloud-based platform, say a platform-as-a-service provider, which will work and play well with other components written in Cobol or perhaps C++, which are on-premise. Same goes for persistence layers, middleware, protocols, and so on, cloud delivered or on-premise. You can mix and match to exactly meet your needs, even leverage services that may exist outside of your organization without regard for how that service was created, how it communicates, or whether it is running on a cloud or on-premise.

Finally, with this degree of independence, components are protected from each other and can better recover from component failure. If the SOA using cloud computing architecture is designed correctly, the failure of a single component should not take down other components in the system, such as a cloud platform outage stopping the processing of key on-premise enterprise applications. Therefore, loose coupling creates architectures that are more resilient. Moreover, loose coupling also better lends itself to creating failover subsystems, moving from one instance of a component to another without affecting the other components, which is very important when using cloud computing platforms.

It should be noted, however, that not all tight coupling is bad. In some cases, it makes sense to more tightly couple components, such as when the dependencies are critical to the design. An example would be two services that cannot work apart and must function as one, and thus are better tightly coupled—for instance, a transactional service that requires the remote databases to be up and running for the service to work correctly. These services should be tightly coupled, and it is not a bad thing to do so. You have to look at your requirements and determine the degree of coupling required in your architecture, and it may not always be loose coupling.

Are You Loosely Coupled?

Now that we know the basic differences between a tightly and loosely coupled architecture, as well as the advantages, perhaps it is a good idea to break down loose coupling into a few basic patterns: location independence, communication independence, security independence, and instance independence.

- *Location independence* means that no matter where the service exists, the other components that need to leverage the service can discover it within a directory and leverage it through the late binding process. This comes in handy when you are leveraging services that are consistently changing physical and logical locations, especially services outside of your organization that you may not own, such as cloud-delivered resources. Your risk calculation service may exist on-premise on Monday and within the cloud on Tuesday, and it should make no difference to you.

- Dynamic discovery is key to this concept, meaning that calling components can locate service information as needed and without having to bind tightly to the service. Typically, these services are private, shared, or public services as they exist within the directory.

- *Communications independence* means that all components can talk to each other no matter how they communicate at the interface or protocol levels. Thus, we leverage enabling standards, such as Web Services, to mediate the protocol and interface difference.

- *Security independence* is the concept of mediating the difference between security models in and between components. This is a bit difficult to pull off but necessary to any SOA. To enable this pattern, you have to leverage a federated security system that can create trust between components, no matter what security model is local to the components. This is the primary force behind the number of federated security standards that have emerged in support of a loosely coupled model and Web Services.
- *Instance independence* means that the architecture should support component-to-component communications, using both a synchronous and an asynchronous model, and not require that the other component be in any particular state before receiving the request or message. If done right, all of the services should be able to service any requesting component, asynchronously, as well as retain and manage state no matter what the sequencing is.

The need for loosely coupled architecture within your cloud computing solution is really not the question. If you leverage cloud computing correctly, other than in some rare circumstances, you should have a loosely coupled architecture. However, analysis and planning are also part of the mix: Understanding your requirements and how each component of your architecture should leverage the other components of your architecture. Leverage the coupling model that works for you.

Defining Metaservices

Now that we understand the nature of services, classes of services, and even how to access services, the next step is to understand and collect information about services in the problem domain. We can call these *metaservices*, or data about services. Then we will talk about creating a services directory, where the services are documented in detail. This information goes into the services directory leveraged to understand the requirements of our cloud computing architecture.

While we certainly understand the use of metadata, or data about data, lately in the modern world of application integration, we have seen the same need to better define information around services existing in an SOA or an SOA using cloud computing. If you think about it, it is a logical step. While we need to keep track of semantics, validation constraints, formats, and so on, around data, we have the same needs in terms of how we manage, understand, and track services.

Behavior (the core value of services) is a notion very different from information. Behavior is much more "living and breathing" than data and provides not only information but dynamic and complex services around that data. This is why we leverage services as well as data for integration. There is, however, no standard approach to describing services at a higher level. With the public nature of services these days, as well as the rate of service replication and abstraction, this should be on the top of our to-do list.

With the advent of Web Services, we now have thousands, sometimes tens of thousands, of services under our management (private services). To make matters even more complex, we also have to consider services that are out of our direct control: those shared from cloud computing platforms (public services). While we do have some basic information about them, as defined by standards such as Web Services Description Language, we really need a more complete set of information surrounding the services. This information should include the purpose, interfaces, parameters, rules, logic, owner, semantics, included services, and other important data. We can define these attributes within the services directory, which we define next.

Creating the Services Directory

Using the previously defined concept of metaservices, let's now explore how to document those services for the purposes of our SOA using cloud computing architecture. Earlier in this chapter, we defined the need to create a list of candidate services as well as to create a final services model, using our case study as an example. Now we look at the concept of a services directory, which is basically a directory of services that you discover, identify, and define as you gain a service-level understanding of your problem domain, and look to replatform some of these services for cloud computing. We know by now that we need the following in our services directory:

- Semantics
- Purpose
- Authentication
- Dependencies
- Service levels

However, we need to add some other important categories, including

- Owner
- Enabling technology
- Programming model
- Performance attributes
- Data validation
- Services leveraged within this service
- Where this service is leveraged
- Function points/object points
- Flow diagram
- Structure charts
- Interface definitions
- Code revisions
- Test plans
- Test results
- Development tools (include version)

What exactly is a service directory? It is a database of information, a repository, about service, including the properties just described. Although many experts view repositories primarily as a part of the world of application development and data warehousing, they do not question their value to the world of enterprise architecture and our ability to track services that extend out to cloud-delivered platforms.

We create the services directory as a way to drive through our process, including the creation of the services and information model, as well as the final service model. Creating the directory is a way to understand the services and the information bound to the services in detail. The services directory becomes the starting point for the SOA repository. It can be passively defined, not dynamically interacting with the services, or actively defined, meaning that the repository is in direct interaction with the services, both on-premise or cloud delivered.

The goal is to provide a sophisticated directory that can keep track of a good deal more than the rudimentary information (such as directory data). It should track more sophisticated information about services in the problem domain. The directory should provide all the information required by the architect and programmer to locate any piece of information within the on-premise or cloud platforms and to link it to any other piece of information.

The directory must be the master directory for the entire architecture spanning on-premise and the clouds, which eventually becomes the registry.

In more sophisticated cloud computing solutions, the services directory is becoming the *axis mundi*, able to access both the source and target systems in order to discover necessary information (such as metadata and available business processes). Engaged in this "autodiscovery," the SOA solution can populate the directory with this or any other information that may be required. Ultimately, the services directory will become the enterprise metadata repository, able to track all systems, services, and information, on-premise or on the cloud-delivered platforms.

The value of a services directory should be clear. With the directory as a common reference point for all connected processes, services, and databases, integrating data and services is straightforward. The services directory can also track the rules that the architect and developer apply within the SOA problem domain.

Consider Service Governance

One of the things that is often forgotten when looking at SOA using cloud computing is the notion of services governance, which is covered more extensively in Chapter 8, "Bringing Governance to the Clouds." From SOA governance, service governance is basically the same concept, or the ability to track, manage, and control the use of services that span on-premise and cloud-based systems.

There are two types of service governance: design time and runtime.

Design time service governance, as the name implies, typically provides an integrated registry/repository that attempts to manage a service from its design to its deployment, but typically not during runtime execution of the services, albeit some do.

Key components of design time service governance include

- A registry and/or repository for tracking service design, management, policy, security, and testing artifacts
- Design tools, including service modeling, dependency tracking, policy creation and management, and other tools that assist in the design of services

- Deployment tools, including service deployment, typically through binding with external development environments
- Links to testing tools and services, providing the developer/designer the ability to create a test plan and testing scenarios and then to leverage service-testing technology

In essence, design time service governance works up from the data to the services, gathering key information as it goes. You typically begin by defining the underlying data schema and turning that into metadata and perhaps an abstraction of the data. Then, working up from there, you further define the services that interact with the data, data services, and then transactional services on top of that. You can further define that into processes or orchestration. All this occurs with design time information managed within the design time service governance system.

Runtime service governance works and plays in the world of service management and should be linked with design time service governance, but often is not. Design time is all about defining the policies around the use of services. Therefore, runtime governance is the process of enforcing and implementing those policies at service runtime, but it may do other things as well.

Runtime service governance, like design time service governance, comes in many flavors because of the number of vendors in that space and how it is defined by that vendor. There are no de facto standards as to what runtime service governance needs to be, but certain patterns are emerging.

Runtime service governance typically includes

- Service discovery
- Service delivery
- Security
- Setting and maintaining appropriate service levels
- Managing errors and exceptions
- Enabling online upgrades and versioning
- Service validation
- Auditing and logging

The Need for a Service-Level Understanding

While we covered a lot in this chapter, the core concept you want to take away is that we need to understand the core services that exist in our problem domain in order to make the right calls around which services should reside on-premise and should exist within a cloud computing platform.

Through this exercise, we have a much better understanding of the interworkings of our applications: what they do, the information they process, which are good candidates for cloud computing, and which are not. Those who choose to skip this process will find that services exist on the wrong platform, either cloud or on-premise, and the new cloud computing architecture is likely to fail.

While this seems like a lot of work, it really is only a quick survey and understanding of the present services. While we recommend basic concepts and basic approaches, the needs of your IT environment are going to be unique and may require slightly different approaches. As long as the objective of having a complete understanding of the services within the problem domain are achieved, the way you go about doing that project is up to you.

Another benefit of understanding the domain at a services level is that you can easily leverage the work defined in this chapter in other directions, perhaps to support the core enterprise architecture or build and/or refine your SOA. As we described at the beginning of this chapter, many of the techniques and concepts are taken directly from SOA, with the caveat that we are looking at SOA as it leverages cloud computing.

The fact of the matter is that most of those looking to leverage cloud computing will skip the approaches defined in Chapters 5, 6, and 7. They will typically start relocating or creating core business processes on cloud computing platforms without a clear understanding of what they are relocating or building. Chances are high that they will fail more often than succeed. With a little bit of architectural planning and some basic work, you can remove a bunch of risk from your cloud computing project. After all, we are looking to reduce risk and cost—otherwise there is no need to consider cloud computing. A little work goes a long way here and could make the difference between a successful cloud computing effort and some of the disasters we are bound to hear about as we move further along with this technology.

CHAPTER 7

Working from Your Processes to the Clouds

A process cannot be understood by stopping it. Understanding must move with the flow of the process, must join it and flow with it.

—Frank Herbert (1920–1986)

Okay, we are moving up the stack. We have an information- or data-level understanding of our problem domain from Chapter 5, "Working from Your Data to the Clouds," and a service-level understanding of our problem domain from Chapter 6, "Working from Your Services to the Clouds." Now we need to look at completing the story by having a process-level understanding—the purpose of this chapter.

This book teaches concepts that help you understand what you are dealing with and how to create a basic architecture that allows you to make decisions about which information, services, and processes, if any, are good candidates for relocating to the clouds. In this chapter, we spend a lot of time talking about the concept of processes and the notion of business process management. These are not necessarily new concepts; we are just looking at them under a new architectural light: SOA and SOA using cloud computing.

This chapter is designed in reverse, making sure to introduce the continuation of our methodology and the basic concepts up front, and then getting into the technical details around business process management at the end of the chapter. This approach provides a better context for that information and ends with a good foundation of what BPM is in the context of cloud computing, SOA, and architecture in general.

Moreover, we are using approaches taken directly from SOA. As you may recall from earlier in the book, we leverage SOA approaches because they provide a great way to break down the architecture to its functional primitive and rebuild it as information, services, and now a process model. Once that is complete, it is much easier to mix and match the architectural components between on-premise and cloud-based systems and place them where they can do the most good and cost the least.

In this chapter, we talk about a *process*, or a sequence of events that leverage services, typically as it relates to the automation of a business process. For the most part, we talk about how these processes are integrated, which is called *business process management*, or *BPM*, although the definition of BPM depends somewhat on who is saying it or what technology leverages the notion. We focus somewhere between the technology and the business concepts for this chapter.

What Is BPM?

BPM may be applied to any number of business events, including

- Processing a customer request
- Manufacturing an automobile
- Delivering a product to a customer
- Processing a financial transaction

In general, BPM logic addresses only process flow and service invocation. It is not traditional programming logic, such as user interface processing, database updates, or the execution of transactions. Indeed, in most BPM scenarios, the process logic is separated from the application logic. It functions solely to coordinate or manage the information flow or invocation of application services between many source and target applications that exist within organizations.

The notion is fairly simple: place a layer of control logic on top of the services and systems that allows the control logic to bind the services into a single, unified, multistep business process that can carry out the unique functions of the business process. It must do so in the correct order; with the proper information, control sequences, state maintenance, and durability; and with the ability handle exceptions (see Figure 7.1).

We create processes using either paper or a graphics drawing tool. However, while these tools enable us to depict the process as a visual drawing, other tools allow us to depict the process graphically and then connect that process with services. While this technology is called by different names, most refer to it as BPM technology, which is typically made up of a

- *Graphic modeling tool* used to create the business model and define behavior.
- *Business process engine* that controls the execution of the multistep business process and maintains state and the interactions with the middleware, which, in turn, interacts with any number of source or target systems.
- *Business process monitoring interface* that allows end users to monitor and control the execution of a business process in real time and optimize where needed.
- *Business process engine interface* that allows other applications to access the business process engine.
- *Integration technology*, or application integration middleware, or anything that facilitates communication with the services.

Process-as-a-Service

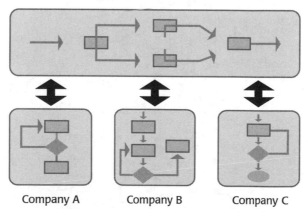

Company A   Company B   Company C

Figure 7.1 Business process management means placing meta-application layers on top of existing processes and services. This figure depicts a process that spans many companies using processes that exist within a cloud-delivered platform.

BPM is a strategy as much as a technology. It strengthens your organization's ability to interact with any number of systems—inside or outside the organization, on-premise or cloud-based—by integrating entire business processes both within and among enterprises or from on-premise to cloud-delivered processes (see Figure 7.2). It is important to consider that processes may span from

- On-premise to cloud-based
- Just cloud-based
- Just on-premise
- Intraenterprise (within a company)
- Interenterprise (between companies)

Processes can span any number of complex systems within the same company or among companies, and can exist and leverage resources that are locally hosted (on-premise) or cloud computing based. This functionality exists to bind services together to create solutions that are easy to create and change. Since processes typically do not drive constant development and redevelopment, BPM is more of a configuration process. The core value is to drive and solve business problems by leveraging processes.

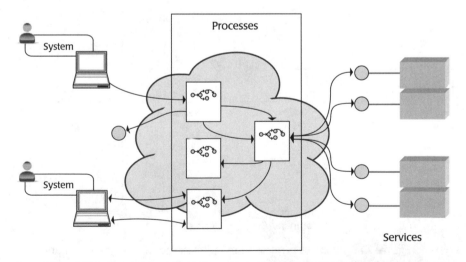

Figure 7.2   BPM allows you to bind services, cloud-based or on-premise, to create core business processes for your business.

BPM deals with several organizations and internal systems using various metadata, platforms, and processes. BPM even deals with people and other non-IT-related entities that may participate in a process, also called workflow. Thus, BPM technology must be flexible, providing a translation layer between the services and the BPM engine. Moreover, BPM technology must work with several types of technologies and interface patterns.

Bringing Process to the Clouds

The larger story is that we are looking to define processes on top of our services to create a model that allows us to best determine which processes should be placed on cloud platforms. Figure 7.3 depicts the current state where processes reside within on-premise systems, with some of them being good candidates to exist on cloud platforms.

Figure 7.4 shows us processes that have been relocated to a cloud-based system, in essence, simply by moving the location where these processes are

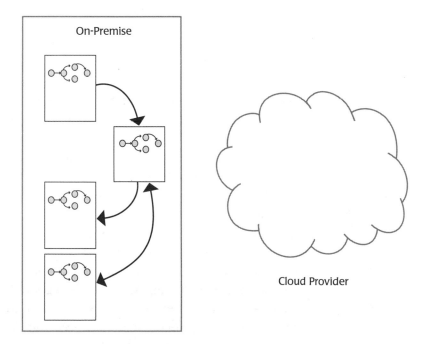

Figure 7.3 Processes exist on-premise and have the potential to become cloud-based processes.

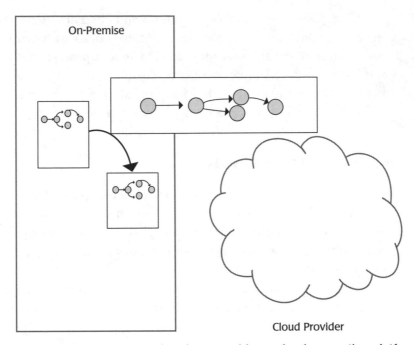

Figure 7.4   Processes, once analyzed, may reside on cloud computing platforms as needed to support the business. Some processes exist on-premise, some in the clouds, and some span both on-premise and cloud-based systems.

hosted, depending on the requirements of the architecture. This is a very simple concept. However, figuring out which processes to move and where to put them is a more complex issue that we cover in more depth in Chapter 10, "Defining Candidate Data, Services, and Processes for the Clouds," and Chapter 11, "Making the Move to Cloud Computing." Keep in mind that while processes need to run someplace, either on-premise or within the clouds, processes are always able to touch services, and sometimes data, that exist anywhere in the architecture, including on-premise and cloud-based platforms. Therefore, they can exist wherever they need to exist, and you can leverage them to bind together all services that are network accessible.

Note that while we can typically host data and services only on single platforms—on-premise or cloud-based—in the world of BPM, we may have processes that span platforms, binding together services and data between cloud-based and on-premise systems. Moreover, these processes can be inter-platform—cloud-based and on-premise—and they can span across many companies, geographies, and other cloud platforms. Potentially dozens of services, data, and processes can be bound together across many internal systems within many companies and many cloud platforms using a single process that may be hosted anywhere.

Defining Processes

How do services fit into the picture? Returning to our services model from Chapter 6 and adding processes, it is clear to see that processes connect services together to solve business problems, and services and processes may reside on-premise or on cloud-based platforms as needed to support the architecture, as seen in Figure 7.5.

Processes are funny things in that they may be services themselves, and services can leverage processes just as processes can leverage services. This is not meant to confuse things, just to point out that both services and processes are able to provide behavior. Processes, as we stated earlier, leverage a configuration and not a programming approach to defining that behavior, so it is much easier to redefine a process than it is to redefine a service.

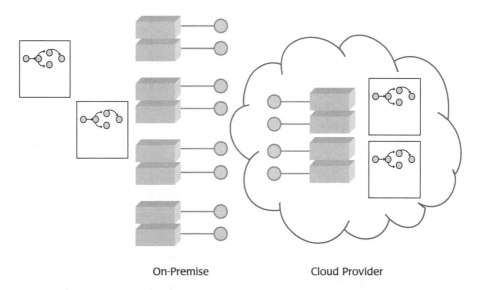

On-Premise   Cloud Provider

Figure 7.5 The general idea. Processes leverage services for behavior and information, and these processes and services can reside on-premise and cloud-based systems as needed to support the architecture.

What must be understood is that data, services, and processes may move between on-premise and cloud-based systems as needed to support the business and the architecture. The trick, and the reason you are reading this book, is to determine which ones should reside where, which we cover extensively in Chapters 10 and 11.

Figure 7.6 depicts our process for defining the process model, which is the next step in our methodology, so we can better understand our problem domain before relocating processes from on-premise systems to cloud-based systems, as needed.

Understand the processes means that we look at the processes within our problem domain that are automated or not automated, define them at a high level, and add them to a list of candidate processes. The idea is that we list pro-

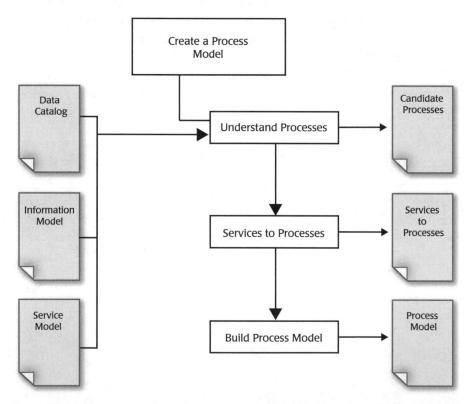

Figure 7.6   The process of creating a process model looks very much like it did in designing the services model in Chapter 6, because services and processes share many of the same patterns. However, processes are different enough from services to require their own steps.

cesses, as we did services, that have the potential of becoming part of our architecture. This is a step toward having a quick understanding of the processes within the problem domain. We must also look at the effectiveness of the existing processes, including which processes should be added, deleted, and changed.

Defining *services to processes* is the step where we bind services, defined in the previous step, to processes. We do this to create processes that are built on existing services, because processes typically do not define information or behavior; they define how we leverage services to form business solutions. Processes should be loosely coupled and easy to configure. Again, we are attempting to place volatility into the domain or processes so we can change these processes through a configuration and reconfiguration exercise, not through reprogramming.

Build the process model is just that: the task of putting together a process model, or the fundamental approach to defining and building processes—the processes that will be part of the to-be architecture. In other words, these are processes we found, the model that depicts how we would like to configure them logically as processes, and how they link back to services, which are linked back to the data. Later, in Chapters 10 and 11, we look at how we want to deploy them and where.

Now let's revisit the case study we have been working through in the last couple of chapters. As you may remember, we defined the data and the candidate services for the General Ledger system:

General Ledger Database
Customers
CNum (char 30)
CName (char 30)
CAddress (char 40)
CCity (char 30)
CZip (char 5)

Products
PNum (char 30)
PDesc (char 40)
PPrice (num 10)

Sales
CNum (char 30)
PNum (char 30)
SAmount (num 10)

Candidate services for the General Ledger system are

Add_Customer
Del_Customer
Update_Customer
Add_Account
Update_Account
Add_Product
Del_Product
Update_Product
Record_Sales
Update_Sales

Now we want to abstract or create processes from these services. Assuming that the processes will not span outside of the existing General Ledger system, a single process for generating a customer record might look like this:

1. Generate_Customer_Record
   1.1. Add_Customer
   1.2. Add_Account
   1.3. Record_Sales

So, we would move from Add_Customer to Add_Account, and then finally to Record_Sales, invoking each service in sequence, perhaps having control logic and exception handling as part of the process. While this is a very simple procedure, the core concept of BPM exists here, including the ability to sequence the use of services, stringing them together to form a process. We provide other examples later in this chapter.

It is important that you keep these steps in mind as you read the rest of the chapter. This approach not only defines the concept of processes within the context of the cloud computing opportunity, but helping you to understand the approach before we get into the technical nitty-gritty is a much better way to learn.

SOA, Agility, and Processes

Processes are core to the value of SOA; the ability to place things that will change over time into a configuration (or BPM) layer makes it easier to change key business processes. Cloud computing platforms are just places where those processes and services may reside—an architectural option.

Thus, the core notion here is about placing things that may or will change over time into the process configuration layer and addressing things that will probably not change as services. For instance, the addition of a new product line may cause the way the company defines sales tax to change. Using processes, we can make that change as a configuration to a process and not force redevelopment of enterprise systems. This means that the architecture is better able to support change, which brings the value of agility to IT (for more information on defining the value for your enterprise, see the Book Blog on the next page).

While SOA was initially sold around the value of reuse, or the ability to reuse services among various systems, users have come to discover that the real value that SOA provides is the ability to change core business processes without requiring waves of redevelopment, testing, and deployment. This is a very important point—perhaps one of the most important points of this chapter.

Agility has proven more valuable than reuse when considering the value of SOA. In a recent study published in *Information Week* entitled "InformationWeek Analytics: State of SOA," it was found that that the value of reuse is only marginal:

> The percentage of overall software reuse within organizations was only marginally higher after initiating SOA, with a 32% reuse rate cited before the SOA project versus 39% after.[1]

Thus, the value proposition around SOA is the ability to promote an agile architecture, or an architecture that is built to change. If we keep this objective in focus, the business value becomes apparent, considering the value of accommodating the needs of the business in a much timelier manner.

---

1. Roger Smith, "InformationWeek Analytics: State of SOA," February 21, 2009. Available at http://www.informationweek.com/news/industry/other/showArticle .jhtml?articleID=214501922.

Value of Agility via Processes

Considering the value of agility, process configuration is a core tenet of SOA and its application to cloud computing. It is a good exercise to determine the value of agility for your business or project in order to better define your own needs, make a business case for the SOA project, and set the appropriate expectations for the value of moving to cloud computing through SOA approaches.

What is the value of agility? Agility is a strategic advantage that is difficult, but not impossible, to measure in hard dollars. We first need to determine a few things about the business, including

- The degree of change over time
- The ability to adapt to change
- Relative value of change

The degree of change over time is really the number of times over a particular period that the business reinvents itself to adapt to a market. While a paper production company may have a degree of change of only 5% over a 5-year period, a high-technology company may have an 80% change over the same period. Thus, agility has value, but different value based on what the business is and does.

The ability to adapt to change can be expressed as a number (that you determine) that states the company's ability to react to the need for change over time. The notion is that the use of a process configuration solution allows you to make many changes to the core business processes, typically without driving change to the underlying services and data.

Finally, the relative value of change is the amount of money made as a direct result of changing the business, such as a retail organization's ability to establish a frequent-buyer program to react to changing market expectations and the resulting increases in revenue from making that change.[2]

---

2. David S. Linthicum, "SOA Meets ROI." Presentation to the Open Group, July 2004. https://www.opengroup.org/conference-live/uploads/40/10289/Wed_-_pm_-_1_-_Linthicum.pdf.

Value of BPM for the Clouds

What does BPM bring to the cloud computing table? It is really another complete layer on the stack, over and above on-premise or cloud-based systems. Or, to be more specific:

- A single instance of BPM typically spans many instances of systems, on-premise or cloud-based.
- BPM defines a master application (or applications) that has visibility into many encapsulated services and information.
- BPM leads with a process model, moves information among applications, and invokes internal services in support of that model.
- BPM is independent of the services. Changes can be made to the processes without having to change the source or target systems, on-premise or cloud-based.
- BPM is strategic, leveraging business rules to determine how systems should interact and better leverage the business value from each system through a common abstract business model.

Let's walk through a simple example. Let's say you want to build a model airplane, and you have three main processes:

1. The process of cutting the parts.
2. The process of assembling the parts.
3. Finishing the airplane (painting and attaching the decals).

These are the higher-level processes; of course, many processes will be contained inside these processes.

In the terms of BPM, we can define the three main processes as

1. Cut parts.
2. Assemble parts.
3. Finish airplane.

And we have to build these processes on top of three source and target systems:

1. Inventory (SAP; on-premise)
2. Sales (Salesforce.com; application-as-a-service, storage-as-a-service)
3. Manufacturing (Amazon AWS; information-as-a-service)

Using these assumptions, we could define "Cut parts" as a process that is kicked off by a sales event from the sales system that is posted to the manufacturing system. We can then decompose that "Cut parts" process down to additional subprocesses if needed (we are not going to do that here). After the parts are cut, we let manufacturing know that the process is complete, and it in turn kicks off the process to assemble the parts. Once that is complete, we return information to the manufacturing system, and it kicks off the finishing processing. Once that occurs, the inventory system is updated with the information on the completed product, and the sales system is updated with the fact that the product is complete and ready for shipment.

The key idea is that the higher-level processes, the meta-application in a sense, drive the processes and coordinate the exchange of information between the source and target systems. These processes leverage service interfaces and abstract the encapsulated processes up to a higher-level set of processes in support of this business event.

Although this is a very simplistic example, it is nonetheless a good depiction of the higher-level activities and concepts of BPM.

BPM is the science and mechanism of managing the movement of data and the invocation of services in the correct and proper order to support the management and execution of common processes that exist in and between organizations and internal applications. BPM provides another layer of easily defined and centrally managed processes that exist on top of an existing set of processes, application services, and data within any set of applications.

The goal of our discussion is to define a mechanism to bind relevant processes that exist between internal and external systems in order to support the flow of information and logic between them, thus maximizing their mutual value. Moreover, we are looking to define a common, agreed-upon process that exists between many organizations, has visibility into any number of integrated systems, and is visible to any system that needs to leverage the common process model.

Understanding the Semantics

As we move into the world of BPM, we find that the names for particular types of technologies and approaches can be somewhat confusing. As we mentioned earlier in this chapter, no standard definitions exist for these concepts, so perhaps it is time we created them.

- *Business process automation (BPA)* tools and approaches provide mechanisms for the automation of business processes without end-user interaction at execution time. Most application integration tools provide this type of subsystem.
- *Workflow* tools allow for the automation of business processes with end-user interaction (typically) at execution time. These categories of technology and approaches are typically document oriented, moving document information among human decision makers.
- *BPM* is an aggregation of business process modeling, business process automation, and workflow. This approach implements and manages transactions and real-time business processes that span multiple applications, providing a layer to create common processes that span many processes in integrated systems.

The good news is that most business processes are already automated. The bad news is that they tend to exist within different systems. For example, adding a customer to a packaged accounting application may establish the customer in that system, but it may still be necessary to use another system (a different system that may exist within a trading partner) to perform a credit check on that customer and still another system to process an invoice. You need not possess exceptional insight to recognize the potential for disaster that exists in this scenario. Not only do these disparate systems need to share information and services, but they also need to share that information in an orderly and efficient manner.

The goal of BPM, and the use of BPM within cloud computing, is to automate services invocation and process flow so that another layer of processes will exist over and above the processes encapsulated in existing systems. In other words, BPM completes application binding, allowing the integration of systems by readily sharing information and services and by managing the sharing of that information and services with easy-to-use tools. This enables the process architect to create and re-create processes to solve business problems and adjust processes as needed, as the business changes.

Drilling Down on BPM

BPM is best defined as applying appropriate rules in an agreed-upon, logical multistep sequence in order to leverage information among participating systems and to visualize and share application services, including the creation of a common abstract process that spans both internal and external systems. This definition holds true regardless of whether or not the business processes are automated.

The use of a common process model that spans multiple systems and companies for application integration provides many advantages, including

- *Modeling*, or the ability to create a common, agreed-upon process among computer systems, either on-premise or cloud-based, automating the integration of all information systems to react in real time to business events such as increased consumer demand, material shortages, and quality problems.
- *Monitoring*, or the ability to analyze all aspects of the business and enterprise or trading community to determine the current state of the process in real time.
- *Optimization*, or the ability to redefine the process at any given time in support of the business and thus make the process more efficient.
- *Abstraction*, or the ability to hide the complexities of the local applications from the business users and have the business users work with a common set of business semantics.

There are three types of processes to visualize enterprise and cross-enterprise processes: internal, shared, and specialized processes.

- *Internal processes* exist at the intracompany level, allowing the business user to define common processes that span only systems that are within the enterprise and are not visible to the trading partners or to community-wide processes. For example, the process of hiring an employee may span several systems within the enterprise but should not be visible to processes that span an enterprise or trading community or other organizations. When considering cloud computing, the internal processes may span on-premise or cloud-based systems, but they are internal nonetheless.
- *Shared processes* exist between companies and consist of a set of agreed-upon procedures for exchanging information and automating business processes within a community. These are good candidates for processes that should be hosted on cloud computing platforms.

- *Specialized processes* are created for a special requirement, such as collaboration on a common product development effort that exists only between two companies and has a limited life span. These processes are created to address a specific need and will be removed at some point.

Abstraction of business applications, cloud or on-premise, into a BPM solution requires the removal of flow dependency from the application. The routing feature found in most BPM solutions allows relevant information to be extracted from any service. The advantage of this solution is that only the model itself needs to be altered when a change in process flow or logic is required. There is no need to change the applications that are part of the process model. In addition, this approach allows reuse of any source or target system from model to model.

BPM and Cloud Computing

The science around the use of processes in the context of architectural patterns such as SOA, and the use of cloud computing as an architectural option, is going to drive a lot of the value of cloud computing. What is needed is a centralized control mechanism that allows you to take full advantage of the resources, such as services and data, that exist on any platform, on-premise or cloud-based, turning them into business solutions.

The larger value is that, once the resources are defined as processes, you can change these processes using a configuration and not a reprogramming approach. This allows you to alter the architecture around the changing needs of the business, cloud computing or not.

The migration toward cloud computing will highlight the use of BPM as we seek to manage many heterogeneous systems that may exist anywhere in the world, binding them together as a set of processes made up of many things that support the business. We may shortly see a world with dozens of systems, on-premise and cloud-based, that may support a single process spanning many companies, countries, and platforms. The use of processes will be the single architectural component that binds them together.

Thus, the concept of processes that reside in the clouds is not as much about looking at processes that are good candidates for placing on cloud computing platforms as it is about looking at processes in general and how they will span between cloud computing–delivered platforms and our enterprise.

CHAPTER 8

Bringing Governance to the Clouds

*How can you govern a country that
has 246 varieties of cheese?*

—Charles De Gaulle (1890–1970)

It is Tuesday morning. You just got a page from the vice president of sales that the customer relationship management (CRM) system is down—again. You look into the issue and find that your cloud computing provider has altered a database update service, which made your customer information access processes fail, which stopped the CRM system. You had no idea the service was going to change and no idea how the change in that service would affect the other enterprise systems. In other words, you lack governance, or the ability to control changes to services and the usage of services.

Cloud computing needs governance in order to be successful. If you think about it, at the end state of our architecture we have thousands of services and data elements under management, and we must control how they are accessed, added, deleted, and altered. We need an approach, processes, procedures, and technology—we need governance.

In the world of enterprise architecture, governance means control, or the ability to mandate the use of standards and approaches, almost a management concept. In the world of SOA , simply put, governance means designing, building, testing, and implementing policies for services and monitoring their use.

Governance as related to services, or service governance, is most applicable to the use of cloud computing, since we are basically defining our architecture as a set of services that are relocatable between on-premise and cloud computing-based systems. SOA is the approach here, and SOA or service governance is the approach and the technology we leverage to manage the services within the enterprise and cloud.

Policies in the context of SOA and cloud computing are declarative electronic rules about what can be done to a service and by whom:

- Who can access the service.
- What they can do to the service.
- How changes to the service affect other services.
- How changes to the service affect applications.
- How governance works with security.
- How governance links into service testing.
- How governance works with service discovery.
- How governance works with service delivery.
- How to set and maintain appropriate service levels.
- How to manage errors and exceptions.
- How to enable online upgrades and versioning.
- How to perform service validation.
- How to perform auditing and logging.

This is a complete approach and system to make sure the deployed services do what they should do and are monitored and controlled from a single centralized utility: service governance. Service governance is the concept, the approach, and the technology. In this chapter, we introduce the concept of service governance, suggest an approach toward service governance (see Figure 8.1), and provide an understanding of service governance technology.

In Chapter 6, "Working from Your Services to the Clouds," we learned the basics of SOA governance, including the two larger categories, runtime and design time.

Design time service governance typically provides an integrated registry/repository that attempts to manage a service from its design to its deployment but typically not during runtime execution of the services, albeit some do. We do not focus on design time in this chapter or in the book, but we focus on how to design services.

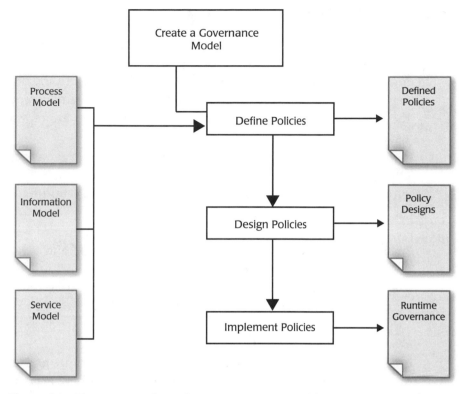

Figure 8.1 The process of creating a governance model involves taking the process, information, and service model built in the previous chapters, then defining, designing, and implementing policies to support governance for cloud computing.

Runtime service governance is the process of enforcing and implementing those policies at service runtime. In essence, runtime service governance is the process of creating policies for services and implementing them on a service governance platform that monitors and controls the services while executing. The importance of doing this in hybrid cloud computing/enterprise architectures becomes obvious as you complete this chapter.

The objective of this chapter is to continue to define our approach, this time defining the process of creating the governance model (see Figure 8.1). Keep in mind that there are entire books on governance as related to enterprise architecture as well as on SOA governance. This chapter does not look to replace those but to provide you with a rudimentary understanding of the concepts and a basic plan for attacking governance as related to your cloud computing efforts.

People and Processes

People and processes, not just technology, make service governance work. The most effective way to implement service governance for cloud computing is to focus on the education of those who will use both the on-premise and cloud computing systems and on how to properly maintain and control them, including what must be done in terms of processes around the governance model.

If you do not consider the people aspect of governance, your governance efforts will fail. So keep in mind that service governance is about people and processes (see Figure 8.2) as much as it is about the concepts of governance and the governance technology.

The problem with governance is that those who are tasked with implementing governance have a tendency to skip the people and the processes and to focus more on the governance technology. Why? Because the people and the processes are hard, and the technology is easy. However, without the support of the people who will build, control, and monitor the cloud computing and on-premise systems, the technology layers in your systems for control simply will not work.

The cloud providers must also participate in governance and work with your on-premise service governance procedures and technology to make this all work. In the example at the beginning of this chapter, the cloud computing provider would have to participate in the service governance processes and procedures in order to let those who leverage the cloud computing plat-

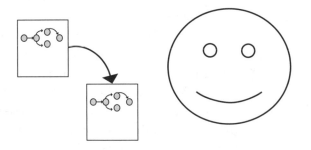

Successful Governance = Processes and People

Figure 8.2 Governance is successful only when you consider the people and the processes.

form know that a service was changing. You can consider this a dance that includes those charged with designing and building the architecture, those who operate the systems within the enterprise, and those who operate the systems within the clouds. If they do not all come together on service governance, it simply will not work no matter what technology you leverage or how good it is.

Governance for the Clouds

We do governance for the simple reason that once we get to a certain number of services, we will not be able to keep track of them all and provide the control they require. Those who build SOA call this the "tipping point," or the point at which the number of services under management becomes so high that it is impossible to manage them properly without a governance model, approach, and service governance technology.

The number of services, as well as the complexities around using those services within the context of cloud computing, makes service governance even more compelling; they include

- Location of the services
- Service dependencies
- Service monitoring
- Service security

Many of the services are not hosted and owned by the business; they are cloud-based, so controls must be placed around them to mediate the risks. What is important when leveraging on-premise SOAs is even more important in the world of cloud computing. In essence, we use the "trust but verify" model, placing a layer of processes and technology around the services so that every event, such as a change to services or a service failure, is quickly known, allowing us to take corrective action or perhaps allowing the technology to self-correct (see Figure 8.3).

When considering the end-state architecture as a combination of SOA and cloud computing, we are looking to build a series of services that are formed and reformed to build business solutions. The services may exist on-premise or may be cloud delivered, but the use of those services by applications and processes, as well as their location, should be completely transparent to the service consumer.

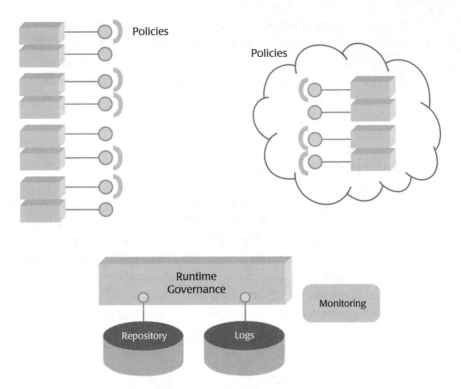

Figure 8.3   Governance means controlling access to service using policies, tracking services using repositories, and logging and monitoring the execution of those services.

Thus, we create something that has a tremendous amount of value when it comes to agility and the ability to operate enterprise IT at greatly reduced costs. However, the architecture is very complex and needs a specialized service governance mechanism to manage this complexity.

Dependencies, as reflected in our opening example, mean that many of these services are interdependent: services call other services, which make them composite services. Moreover, many applications are dependent on these services (see Figure 8.4).

Services that fail or, more likely, that change without authorization have a domino effect on other services and applications that leverage them. A single service that is altered without the knowledge and understanding of the impact that change may have could bring down many core enterprise systems, perhaps costing thousands of dollars an hour in lost revenue, which

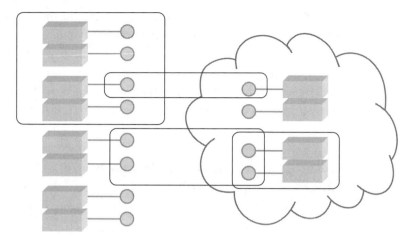

Figure 8.4 Dependencies among applications and services mean that when services fail or are changed, they bring down other services that are coupled to the failed or changed service.

quickly diminishes the value of cloud computing. The use of service governance approaches and technology mitigates the risks.

Operational monitoring means that we place controls around the services through the use of policies, and we can monitor the services, on-premise or cloud delivered, during runtime. What's core here is that you understand what needs to be monitored and at what granularity.

Since there is a performance impact of service monitoring, it is important that you monitor only those services that are critical to the operations of the business. You must make sure they are up and running, and that they provide the performance required by the other services and applications that leverage them. Keep in mind that the overall system runs only as fast as the slowest component.

Monitoring services can be a bit tricky within a cloud computing offering, since you typically do not own the services or the monitoring interfaces to those services. What the cloud computing provider exposes to you is what you get. While providers may allow you to leverage their "monitoring console," you may not be able to monitor their systems down to the service level. You need to consider that limitation as you select a cloud computing provider, making sure you have the ability to monitor those services and can monitor them at the proper level of granularity.

Granularity means we look at the services to be monitored and how deeply we can go, or should go, in that monitoring. While some services need only a "live/dead" status, others may need to have their performance closely monitored, including database and CPU utilization and perhaps other attributes of the service. Moreover, the data needs to be provided as a service so that it may be integrated into your local governance solution.

Governance Interfaces Need Consideration before Selecting a Cloud Computing Provider

Those who implement cloud computing solutions often neglect to consider the points of management for both governance and operational monitoring. Also, many cloud computing providers do not offer them.

In the world of cloud computing, the ability to link to APIs established as interfaces into your cloud computing–based resources allows you to manage those resources as if the resources were local. This provides the capabilities to monitor the health of a service, including performance, up-time, and event logging. Also, on the service governance side of things, you can make sure to control access to the service and specify who is allowed to change it.

However, the ability to combine management-level visibility into cloud computing–based resources varies greatly among providers. Some provide only their own Web page/visual interface for you and cannot link your governance, monitoring, and security solutions at the single-service level. Other do not provide any monitoring at all, arguing that you should just trust them to manage your systems. A few offer well-thought-out management APIs that can seamlessly interact with your service governance and monitoring technologies.

As time goes on, I am sure that monitoring and management interfaces will become more available and more feature rich. For now you need to check into how that cloud provider supports service governance and monitoring. You must consider the level of support when you select your cloud computing provider if you think service governance to be a critical success factor.

Some aspects of security exist in the governance layer. Many existing governance providers also provide basic security services, including the use of identity management, role-based security, service governance, and the ability to support logging and auditing.

A few things must be considered here in terms of security on the context of governance: First, you need to leverage "good enough" security, meaning that the security solution you implement must be appropriate for the application and information you are protecting. Many who implement security tend to go overboard with the security approaches and technology they look to leverage, selecting a solution that is too expensive and places too many limitations on the users.

Second, create your security approach using use cases, looking at how security needs to exist at every level of the system. Sometimes, those who design security, as related to governance, focus more on that last security technology article they read and not enough on how the application needs to leverage security. There is a huge difference.

Creating the Governance Model

Now that we have a basic understanding of service governance, let's return to the creation of our governance model as outlined in Figure 8.1. We create this governance model for a few core purposes: first, to work from the general notion of governance as related to our problem domain to the specifics of the implementation, such as designing and implementing policies. We start from the most general and move to the most specific. Second, to make sure we have a complete service-level, information-level, and process-level understanding of the problem domain, and how all of those assets should be governed, both on-premise and within the cloud computing assets.

Define Policies

Policies, as related to governance, are declarative electronic rules that define the correct behaviors of the services. They can be rules that are not electronically enforced, such as policies created by IT leaders who create rules that everyone must follow but that are not automated. Or, they can be policies outlining proper behavior during service execution, typically enforced electronically using governance technology. Both are important, which is why we discuss policies as things that may exist inside or outside of governance technology.

For our purposes, we call general policies *macro policies* and service-specific policies *micro policies*.

Macro Policies

Macro policies are those policies that IT leaders, such as the enterprise architect, typically create to address sweeping issues that cover many services, the data, the processes, and the applications. Following are examples of macro policies:

- All metadata in both on-premise and cloud computing–based systems must adhere to an approved semantic model.
- All services must return a response in 0.05 seconds for on-premise and 0.10 for cloud computing–based services.
- Changes to processes have to be approved by a business leader.
- All services must be built using Java.

The idea is that we have some general rules that control how the system is developed, redeveloped, and monitored. Macro policies exist as simple rules or set processes that must be followed. For example, there could be a process to address how the database is changed, including 20 steps that must be followed, from initiation of the change to acceptance testing. Another example is the process of registering a new user on the cloud computing platform.

Some IT folk may roll their eyes at the kinds of controls placed around automation. I am sure many such controls exist within your IT shop now. The same people may also push back on extending these governance concepts to cloud computing. However, the core value of implementing macro policies is to reduce risk and save money.

The trick is to strike a balance between too many macro policies, which can hurt productivity, and too few, which can raise the chance that something bad will happen. Not an easy thing, but a good rule of thumb is that your IT department should spend approximately 5% of its time dealing with issues around macro policies. If you spend more time than that, perhaps you are overgoverning. Less than that, or if disaster after disaster happens, perhaps you can put in more macro policies to place more processes around the management of IT resources, on-premise or cloud computing-based.

Micro Policies

Micro, or service-based, policies typically deal with a policy instance around a particular service, process, or data element. They are related to macro policies in that macro policies define what needs to be done, whereas micro policies define how a policy is carried out at the lowest level of granularity. Following are examples of micro policies:

- Only those from Human Resources can leverage Get_Sal_Info services.
- No more than one application, service, or process at a time can access the Update_Customer_Data service.
- The Sales_Amount data element can be updated only by the database administrator, and not by the developers.
- The response time from the get_customer_credit service must be less than 0.0001 seconds.

Micro policies are very specific and typically destined for implementation within service governance technology that can track and implement these types of policies.

Design Policies

Returning to Figure 8.1, policies are designed like any other part of the architecture. The purpose of a policy design is to describe the correct behavior for the service as well as who is allowed access to the service, what they can do with it, and how that access is logged. Finally, a policy defines all other applications, services, processes, and data bound to that service.

While there are design-time governance technologies and approaches, as we discussed in Chapter 6, for the most part, you will design your policies using standard office automation technology. However, you will typically implement your policies by leveraging runtime service governance technology.

You can think of the design component of policies as the process of defining what the policies will do and for what service. Typically, this means listing things that are not allowed, or creating rules. Once the policies are well defined, we implement them using runtime service governance technology, which is the integrated development environment (IDE) and the platform we leverage for policy execution (see Figure 8.5).

Implement Policies

You can consider policies as programs, really. And thus they must be designed, created, tested, and deployed as any program should be. This is the process of implementing policies, which includes testing and deployment.

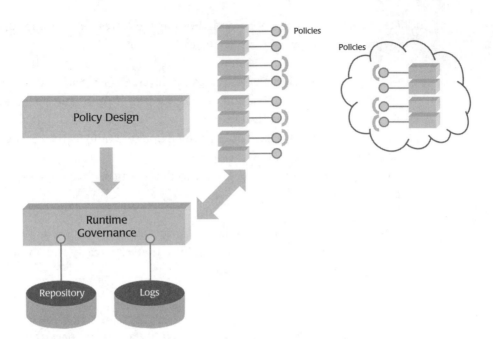

Figure 8.5   We design policies for execution within runtime service governance technology.

Runtime governance technology typically features the ability to test policies; in some cases, specialized testing software is needed. However, policies can be tested during runtime as they execute along with the services on a test platform. The approach and technology you leverage will depend on your requirements.

To test policies effectively, you should create a test plan that outlines how the policy should be tested. Things typically included in a test plan are the definitions of test data, the process of testing the policy, and what defines a policy that is ready for acceptance. The bad news is that you have to create the test plan. The good news is that test plans are typically pretty short for each policy.

Deployment of the policy means moving it into production within the runtime service governance technology or on another platform for executing the policy. Issues to consider for deployment include making sure the platform for policy execution is working as per the requirements. This includes having features in the repository to track the policies, or logging features (see Figure 8.5).

What about Governance in the Cloud?

The idea of governance is to provide command, control, discovery, and monitoring as well as design and development support for services that make up your architecture, including on-premise and cloud-based systems. Most people get that, but in some cases they do not *want* to get that. Perhaps there is a larger opportunity here for both the cloud providers and the end users.

What is so limiting about governance is that you are given an empty registry/repository and asked to fill it up with information about services that you create or, in most cases, expose. From there, it is a constant struggle to keep that repository up to date and to make sure the architecture, cloud and on-premise, is governed properly. We have been here before with metadata repositories that do not seem to get the maintenance they need. Perhaps we are doomed to make the same mistake with cloud governance unless we come up with something clever.

We have dealt with the notion of a shared registry/repository, delivered as a service, for some time now. Instead of leveraging a local repository that just tracks services within your enterprises, you link to a shared repository that already contains thousands of services from thousands of providers, with design and governance information, and it is just a matter of picking what you need and then filling in the gaps with your own services.

This repository would provide not only Web Services Description Language (WSDL) but a complete design-time and runtime governance system delivered out of the cloud, perhaps linked with a local slave repository within your firewall. The core notion would be to provide access and control for both public services, which you and others can leverage, and private services that only your enterprise can see. That would provide a complete governance solution, design-time and runtime, for all services.

Also, since this is a cloud thing, we need to provide "new value." The core value that I see, beyond the use of hosted services you do not develop or maintain, is that design patterns are already defined for you around specific categories of services, and prebuilt policies exist around the operation of those services. These policies, as well as services, are shared: As the services are revised, so are the design artifacts and the policies, both shared and private. In short, you are taking advantage of the community aspect of SOA governance delivered as a service to do most of the work for you—100,000 heads are better than one.

Governance Technology

As you may recall from Chapter 6, runtime service governance technology provides the platform for policy execution and thus the process of enforcing and implementing those policies at service runtime, but it may do other things as well.

Runtime service governance technology comes in many flavors due to the number of vendors in that space and how it is defined by each vendor. There are no de facto standards as to what runtime service governance needs to be, but certain patterns are emerging. Runtime service governance typically includes

- Service discovery
- Service delivery
- Service security
- Setting and maintaining appropriate service levels
- Managing errors and exceptions
- Enabling online upgrades and versioning
- Service validation
- Auditing and logging

Service discovery is the process of finding, analyzing, and detailing an existing service and the defining a policy to govern that service. The great thing about this feature is that you simply enter the location of the service (URL), and the runtime service governance technology does the rest, including entering aspects of the service into the repository (discussed shortly).

Service delivery is the process of moving services from development to execution or production, either on-premise or into the clouds.

Service security encompasses the functions around protection of the managed services and enforcement of the policies.

Setting and maintaining appropriate service levels refers to making sure that all of the services execute per the service agreements and preset levels. This is especially important in an architecture that leverages cloud computing because those services may come with service-level agreements that must be managed too.

Managing errors and exceptions is a feature whereby any errors and exceptions that occur are captured, analyzed, and perhaps recovered from automatically. Typically, this means that those who implement the policies define how errors and exceptions should be managed for a specific service or group of services. The objective is to recover from most errors and exceptions without human intervention, if possible.

Enabling online upgrades and versioning is the process of placing new services and/or policies into service, controlling the process around the upgrades made to services and/or policies, and controlling how services and/or policies are versioned. This is done by allowing the repository to track all services and policies under management, including the complete history of services and policies that have been created, tested, and deployed in either the on-premise or cloud computing–based systems.

As developers build new versions of services, or as policy designers design and build new policies, a mechanism must be in place to insure that updating services and policies will not break the existing system or systems. Runtime service governance is able to track any upgrades that are made, insuring that the applications, processes, and other services leveraging those services are made aware of the change; that alterations are made; and that testing is completed.

Moreover, if issues are discovered, there should be a mechanism to return to the previous version of the service and/or policy. Besides the use of policies to control access to services, this is one of the most important functions of runtime governance.

Service validation, as the name implies, is the feature of the governance technology that validates that the services are "well formed" and prepared to go into production. Service validation asks the question, Is this service valid to the policies and to its expected behavior when in production?

Auditing and logging means that the governance technology will track the execution of the services and the policies, including what they do, when they do it, and who they do it with. This allows those who manage the holistic architecture to analyze auditing and logging information to determine why problems occurred, or better yet, to prevent them. Auditing is required by many legal compliance standards, such as those imposed on public companies or those in regulated vertical markets such as health care.

Governance Dos and Don'ts

Governance is one of those things in the world of SOA and cloud computing that is largely misunderstood. I can understand why: Different vendors define it differently. However, as SOA/cloud computing problem domains become

continued

more complex, typically more than 50 services, the need for governance becomes even more apparent.

How do we select an SOA governance solution? A few dos and don'ts can help with the decision.

Dos

- Do select a vendor that provides governance features that are more runtime in nature. Many governance tools focus on design-time features, which is fine, but the runtime features provide the most value.
- Do look at governance solutions that are well integrated with testing and performance management tools. Let's face it: SOA and cloud computing are performance problems waiting to happen.
- Do make sure to do the upfront planning and place the proper management processes around the technology.

Don'ts

- Don't select a governance vendor only because it is part of a suite of software. It should have value as a standalone product whether it is bundled in a suite of software or not.
- Don't rely on what works for other companies. Your problem domain is unique; the governance solution will be as well. Trust me.
- Don't forget that you and your governance solution will be together for a long time. Consider the quality of the vendor, support, training, and so on. You will find that the better vendors provide holistic value within and beyond the technology.
- Don't marry standards. If there is a fit, great. Don't wait for standards to mature before you move into governance . . . you will be waiting for a very long time.

The Value of Service Governance

We can consider service governance as the ability to define, track, and monitor service execution on any number of platforms, on-premise or cloud computing based. The value of service governance is clear when you consider the amount of risk it removes, since those who manage the systems can be more proactive and get well ahead of issues that will bring down services, which in turn will bring down the systems.

What is important to keep in mind as you drive through your own service governance requirements is that it is not all about technology. People and processes are core issues here as well. Moreover, since we are extending our architecture to the cloud computing platforms, those vendors also need to be involved.

You need a good understanding of the available services, processes, and data at this point before you define service governance approaches, design policies, and deploy them on the service governance technologies. Those who attempt service governance without having that level of understanding do not really know what to govern.

We now have a service, process, information, and service governance understanding of our problem domain. It is time to move on to the next step and the next chapter.

CHAPTER 9

Testing from SOA to the Clouds

Let's just say I was testing the bounds of society.
I was just curious.

—Jim Morrison (1943–1971)

At this point, we have a service-, process-, and information-level understanding of our problem domain, and we have a governance model created as well. Now it is time to explore the unique testing requirements that SOA brings when used with cloud computing. We focus on testing for a few core reasons:

- The mix of on-premise and cloud computing systems and services creates a complex and widely distributed architecture that is also complex to test and requires some new thinking. We are extending our testing to systems we do not own or control. While this is not the first time we have included systems outside of the enterprise within our testing domain, typically, we have never leveraged those systems as vital architectural components. We are breaking some new ground here.
- The testing must occur at many levels, including the user interface, services, governance, processes, and so on, and we need an approach strategy for this multi-level testing requirement.

- There is no single magic testing tool that will solve all of our problems, so we must focus more on the process; technology will not save us here.
- In many instances, this will be your first SOA or your first SOA to leverage cloud computing resources. Your credibility is on the line. Cloud computing or hybrid (on-premise and cloud computing) systems need to function properly out of the gate; otherwise, all of the information provided in this book is for naught.

When we address the architecture in this chapter, we call it what it technically is: *SOA using cloud computing.* The architecture is SOA, which leverages cloud computing resources as part of the architecture. This is the outcome of the process we defined in Chapters 4 through 7.

We focus on testing now because many in IT overlook testing or do not allocate enough resources to properly test their architecture. Testing in the world of cloud computing could cause some additional confusion, since many think that if they neither own nor control cloud computing services, they cannot test them. Nothing could be further from the truth.

If you do not holistically test the services, data, process, and so on, on-premise and within the cloud providers you are leveraging, your systems are not truly tested. If you find issues with the architecture, in many instances they will be issues with your cloud computing provider centered around performance, stability, or perhaps bugs that either you or they introduced in building services and applications on the cloud computing platform. In essence, you need to "test them like you own them," regardless of actual ownership.

This chapter is not a substitute for a complete book on systems testing, and we make sure to recommend a few in the reference section on the book's Web site. The purpose of this chapter is to focus on what is new in the world of testing for SOA using cloud computing, and along with information about the unique aspects of testing this type of architecture, you will find many of the approaches we discuss are based on traditional system testing.

Why We Need a New Take on Testing

Why is SOA and SOA using cloud computing so different that we need a different approach to testing? Many of the same patterns around testing a distributed computing system, such as a SOA, are applicable here. We are not asking you to test much differently but only to consider a few new issues.

There are some clear testing differences to note when cloud computing comes into the mix.

First, we neither own nor control the cloud computing–based systems, so we have to deal with what they provide us, including the limitations, and we typically cannot change it. Thus, we cannot perform some types of testing, such as finding the saturation points of the cloud computing platform to determine the upward limitations on scaling or determining how to crash the cloud computing system. That type of testing may get us a nasty e-mail. White box testing (covered later) of the underlying platform or services (viewing the code), which we can do if we own and control the systems under test, is also not supported by most cloud computing providers.

Second, the patterns of usage, including how one system interacts with another, are different from enterprise to cloud. Traditionally, we test on-premise systems and almost never test a system we cannot see or touch. This includes issues with Internet connectivity.

Third, we are testing systems that are contractually obligated to provide computing service to our architecture, and we need a way to validate that those services are being provided now and into the future. Thus, testing takes on a legal aspect: If the service is not being delivered in the manner outlined in the contract, we can take action.

Finally, cloud computing is new. As such, IT is a bit suspicious about the lack of control. Rigorous and well-defined testing, as described in this chapter, eliminates many of those fears. We must be hyperdiligent to reduce the chances of failure and must work around the fear of change.

Testing from the Enterprise to the Clouds and Back

Testing SOA using cloud computing is a complex, distributed computing problem. We must learn how to isolate, check, and integrate, assuring that things work at the service, persistence, and process layers. The foundation of SOA using cloud computing testing is to select the right tools for the job, have a well-thought-out plan, and spare no expense in testing cycles. Otherwise, our SOA using cloud computing architecture may lay an egg—and there goes our credibility.

Organizations are beginning to roll out their first instances of SOA using cloud computing, typically as smaller projects. While many work fine, some are not living up to expectations because of quality issues that could have been prevented with adequate testing. We need to take these lessons, hard-learned by others, and make sure that testing is high on our priority list.

How Do We Test Architecture?

The answer is, we don't. Instead, we learn how to break the architecture down to its component parts, working from the most primitive to the most sophisticated, testing each component, and then integrating and testing the holistic architecture. In other words, we have to divide the architecture, which in this case is partly on-premise and partly in the clouds, into domains, such as services, security, and governance, and test each domain using whatever approach and tools are indicated. If this sounds complex, it is. The notion of SOA using cloud computing is a loosely coupled complex interdependence, and the approach for testing must follow the same patterns.

White Box and Black Box Testing

We use two major approaches to testing our architecture: black box testing and white box testing.

Black box testing is the process of testing functions into which we do not have complete visibility. For instance, we might ask a system to perform some sort of behavior, such as to return information from an API call, and we would not be able to see what happened inside that system as it accessed the database and processed the information on behalf of the request.

Black box testing is most important when leveraging cloud computing because we typically do not own, control, or have visibility into the inside of a multitenant cloud computing system. Black box testing is the typical approach in an SOA and cloud computing system, and we discuss how to approach black box testing at the end of this chapter.

White box testing, in contrast, allows us to test a system while having complete visibility into the system. When we ask a system to perform some sort of behavior, such as returning information from an API call, we can see how the request is internalized into the program, how the database request is formulated, how the database is accessed, how the information returned from the database is processed . . . you get the idea.

Leveraging white box testing, however, does not mean we can skip black box testing. We still need to verify that the system functions correctly as a whole system, even after we have traced through the code. White box testing is not a replacement for black box testing; it is just another step we can leverage to test the component more completely.

While white box testing is typically optimal, it is not always cost effective. In the case of leveraging cloud computing providers, it is not possible. Understanding black box testing and white box testing, and when and where to leverage each approach, is important as we test our architecture.

As you may recall from Chapter 1, "Where We Are, How We Got Here, and How to Fix It," you can group the testing domains for SOA using cloud computing into these major categories:

- Service-level testing
- Process-level testing
- Governance-level testing
- Information-level testing

We are now adding

- Integration-level testing
- Security-level testing

These are components of the architecture as well.

We focus more on service-level testing, on-premise and cloud-based, because it is most critical to SOA using cloud computing. The categories or domains that you choose to test within your architecture may differ depending on the specific requirements for your architecture. Other areas need attention as well, including quality assurance for the code, performance testing, and auditing.

Service-Level Testing

Within the world of SOA using cloud computing, services are the building blocks. Services become the base of an SOA and can be on-premise or cloud-based. While some are abstract, existing "legacy services," others are new and built for specific purposes, and many more are hosted by cloud computing providers.

Moving up the stack, we find composite services, or services made up of other services, and all services leveraged by the business process or process layer, which provides the agile nature of an SOA using cloud computing, since we can create and change solutions using a configuration metaphor, as we discussed in Chapter 1.

When testing services, keep the following in mind:

- *Services are not complete applications or systems and must be tested as such.* They are a small part of an application. However, they are not subsystems; they are small parts of subsystems as well. They must be tested with a high degree of independence, meaning that the services are able to properly function both by themselves and as part of a cohesive system. Services are analogous to traditional application functions in terms of design and how they are leveraged to form solutions, fine- or coarse-grained.
- *The best approach to testing services is to list the use cases for those services.* Then we can design testing approaches for that service, including testing harnesses, or the use of SOA testing tools that automate testing at the interface and service levels (see Figure 9.1). We must also consider any services the service may employ: they must be tested holistically as a single

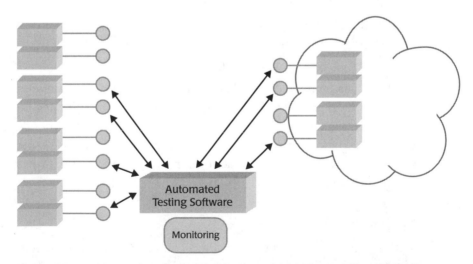

Figure 9.1 Automated testing tools allow services to be tested using preprogrammed scripts and programs that simulate real usage.

logical service. In some cases, we may be testing a service that calls a service that calls a service, where some of the services are developed and managed in-house and some exist on cloud-based systems that we do not control. All use cases and configurations must be considered.

- *Services should be tested with a high degree of autonomy.* They should execute without dependencies, if at all possible, and be tested as independent units of code using a single design pattern that fits within other systems that use many design patterns. While all services cannot be all things to all containers, it is important to spend time understanding their foreseeable use and make sure those are built into the test cases.

- *Services should have the appropriate granularity.* Do not focus on too-fine-grained or too-coarse-grained services. Focus on the correct granularity for the purpose and use within the SOA using cloud computing. The issues related to testing are along the lines of performance more than anything else. Too-fine-grained services have a tendency to bog down because of the communications overhead required when dealing with so many services. Too-coarse-grained services do not provide the proper values to support their reuse. We must work with the service designer as well as developers on this one.

What do we test for within services? It is important to follow a few basic principles.

First, services should be tested for *reuse (reusability)*. Services become a part of any number of other applications and thus must be tested so they properly provide behavior and information but are not application or technology specific. This is a difficult paradigm for many developers, since custom one-off software that digs deeply into native features is what they have used for most of their careers. Thus, the patterns must be applicable to more than a single problem domain, application, or standard, meaning we must have use for our reusable service, and it must be in good working order.

To test for reusability, we create a list of candidate uses for the service—for instance, a shipping service that plugs into accounting, inventory, and sales systems (see Figure 9.2). Then, the service should be consumed by the client, through either a real application (in a testing domain) or a simulator, and the results noted.

In addition, the service should be tested for *heterogeneity*. Web services should be built and tested so there are no calls to native interfaces or platforms.

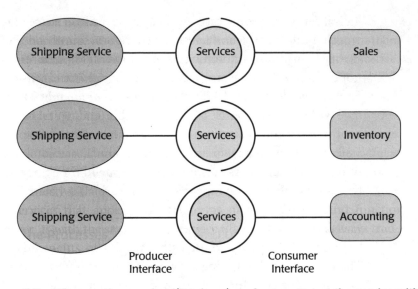

Figure 9.2 When testing services (Producer), make sure to test the service within each application/service (Consumer) where the service will have value within the SOA using cloud computing.

Heterogeneity is necessary because a service, say, one built on Linux, may be leveraged by applications on Windows, Macs, and even mainframes. Those that leverage a service should do so without regard for how it was created and should be completely platform independent. The approach to testing this is rather obvious: Simply consume the service on several different platforms and note any calls to the native subsystems.

Abstraction should also be tested. Abstraction allows access to services from multiple simultaneous consumers, hiding technology details from the service developer. The use of abstraction is required to get around the many protocols, data access layers, and even security mechanisms that may be in place, thus hiding these very different technologies behind a layer that can emulate a single layer of abstraction.

Abstraction is tested effectively by doing, which means implementing instances and then testing the results. Regression and integration testing is the best approach, from the highest to the lowest layers of abstraction.

When we build or design services, we need to test for *aggregation*. Many services will become parts of other services, and thus composite services leveraged by an application, and we must consider that in their design. For instance, a customer validation service may be part of a customer processing service, which is part of the inventory control systems. Aggregations are clusters of services bound together to create a solution; they should be tested holistically through integration testing procedures.

Security-Level Testing

Security strategy, technology, and implementation should be systemic to an SOA using cloud computing, and they bring along new concepts such as identity management. When testing an SOA using cloud computing for security issues, the best approach is to first understand the security requirements and then design a test plan around those requirements, pointing at specific vulnerabilities. Most IT folk are finding that black box testing is the best way to test for security issues in the world of SOA using cloud computing, including penetration testing, vulnerability testing, and so on, using existing techniques and tools.

A further security concern is that an SOA using cloud computing architecture allows services to be consumed outside the enterprise, which creates a new set of vulnerabilities such as information security issues and denial-of-service attacks. We also make the reverse trip, allowing for the consumption of services outside of the firewall. This opens the door for other types of attacks, and the security must be tested in this case as well. Vulnerabilities in this case include malicious services.

Process-Level Testing

As you may recall from Chapter 7, "Working from Your Processes to the Clouds," we can define processes using a standards-based mechanism that defines how Web Services work together, including business logic, sequencing, exception handling, and process decomposition, as well as service and process reuse. Processes may span a few internal systems, systems among organizations, or both. Some processes are long-running, multistep transactions, almost always controlled by one business party, and are loosely coupled and asynchronous in nature.

Processes are really functional services in the context of our architecture. We test them as we do other services, including abstraction, reuse, granularity, and so on. However, note that these processes sit above existing services, and the testing should regress from the top-level services down to the bottom-level services or from the process layer down to the primitive services. Going from the bottom up is the recommended approach.

Governance-Level Testing

As you may recall from Chapter 8, "Bringing Governance to the Clouds," governance requires that you have lifecycle and policy management layers that need testing. No problem. We test governance systems by matching the policies managed and controlled by the governance system with the actual way they manage and control them. It is a simple matter of listing the policies and establishing test cases for each.

Work with the governance technology provider to determine the best approach for testing the governance implemented in the system.

Integration-Level Testing

As with traditional integration testing, the purpose of this step is to figure out if all of the interfaces, including behavior and information sharing between the services, are working correctly. The integration testing should work through the layers of communications, working up through the network to the protocols and interprocess communications, including testing the Representational State Transfer (REST) or Simple Object Access Protocol (SOAP) interfaces to the services or whatever communication mechanism is employed by the services in use.

Following are some things to look for in integration-level testing:

- Can communications be established with late binding, meaning dynamically as needed?
- Is the integration stable under an increasing load?
- Is the transmitted information correct in semantics and content for the service or applications?
- Are the security mechanisms working properly?
- How does the SOA using cloud computing recover from application, database, and network failures?

Information-Level Testing

This is the process of testing the data persistence layers directly, typically the databases, without going through the services. We look at the efficiencies and stability of the database, including

- Performance
- Stability
- Interface efficiencies
- Schema efficiencies

Performance is simply looking to make sure that the database responds to the database requests in an amount of time that meets the needs of the architecture, in this case, the services, and the needs of those invoking the services. Performance issues may be CPU or other computing resource–related, but in many instances there are issues with the design of the database. Keep in mind that information-level testing involves on-premise and cloud computing–based databases.

Stability is testing the database's ability to remain functional for a long period of time. If it fails under an increased load, then we have issues that must be addressed.

Interface efficiencies means we look at the API the database employs to request data, update schemas, and manage the database. These are typically proprietary to the database and should be tested using use cases describing how the interfaces are leveraged in the course of operations.

Finally, *schema efficiencies* concern how well the database is normalized or designed and the ability for that design to service the needs of the architecture. Overnormalized databases can have performance problems, and databases that are not properly normalized can be less effective in serving the services and the architecture as a whole.

Creating a Test Plan

The test plan you create for your architecture should reflect the requirements of your project, and, unfortunately, one size does not fit all. Figure 9.3 depicts the high-level process you can employ to drive SOA using cloud computing testing for your project. However, you may have special needs, perhaps more emphasis on certain architectural components, such as performance and security. You must adjust the process accordingly.

At the end of the day, you will find that SOA using cloud computing testing incorporates all of the testing technology and approaches we have developed over the years for other distributed systems and adds some new dimensions, such as services, processes, and governance testing.

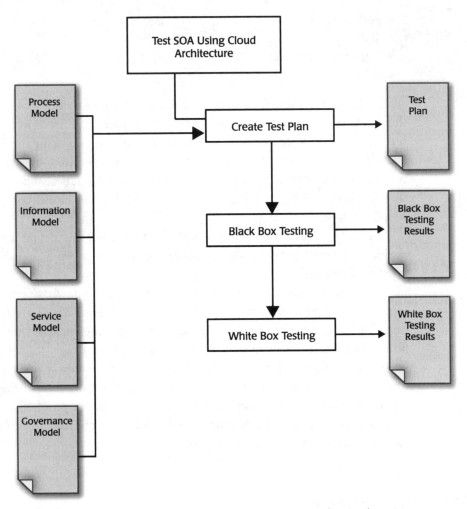

Figure 9.3 A typically high-level SOA using cloud computing testing process.

Black Box Cloud Testing

As we discussed, a portion of SOA using cloud computing is the testing of services we do not host and may not control, or cloud computing–based services. These services are as important to the core systems as the services internal to the application. However, we can remove some of that risk by putting procedures and tools in place to make remote service testing effective enough to determine both the quality of the service and the service levels it will live up to.

Within service-level testing, we can further break them down into two major categories, local and remote services. Local services are services coupled to the core applications and are owned and operated by the enterprise. Remote services, in contrast, are services that exist outside of the domain of the core systems, perhaps within another division within a company or, more likely, leveraged from cloud computing providers as remote Web Services or virtual services.

When considering testing remote services,

- Black box testing is almost always the testing method we use. We have to approach remote services as assets that we cannot change and cannot view beyond the core functionality.
- We do not own the service, so we typically cannot change the service. The services become part of a core system or an SOA using cloud computing, and we have to trust that the service will function correctly; we do so through verification and validation testing.
- We have to consider, when thinking about both testing and security, that we are sharing the remote service with others, typically other enterprises.
- We have to consider service-level agreements (SLAs) within the context of the testing we do. How does the service live up to these SLAs? What are the issues, if any? How do we return results that will make resolution of the issues easiest?

As discussed in Chapter 6, "Working from Your Services to the Clouds," the idea of services is to create a standard interface, programming model, description language, and directory that allows sharing to happen in and between very different systems. Today we can leverage services using cloud computing that are functionally equivalent to the services being hosted locally.

The core value is the ability to mix and match "outside-in" services for use within enterprise applications. However, doing so creates a testing dilemma when we consider the complexity of this architecture, and our ability—or inability—to see into and influence the remote service.

From Chapter 6 we understand the common design patterns of services and the notion of coupling versus cohesion that we must follow. Now the question is: How do we test a service, typically through a black box?

1. Create the test plan, and make sure to define the purpose of the service. What will the service do, and who is the intended user: human, application, other services? From there, we must define input, output, performance

expectations, and so on, for all remote services that will be under test and for the consumers of those services. This is a test plan for a complex distributed system in which the remote services have to be black box tested, so many of the same disciplines, tools, and techniques apply here.

2. Determine the information to be bound to the service, including both metadata and schemas. This means understanding how information is leveraged by the service, what functions require what data, and how to test those functions. Most services are data oriented (data services), so we should consider them data interfaces. We use many of the same testing tools and approaches used to test call-level interfaces and data-oriented APIs.

3. Determine the functions (methods) encapsulated inside the service; in other words, the behaviors we would like to expose, and create testing harnesses for those features. It is also at this step that we define each function, including how the function breaks down using a traditional functional decomposition chart, and make sure to regress through that hierarchy during testing—if indeed we can determine that structure. This can be a bit tricky when black box testing, but not impossible.

4. Identify any interfaces into the service, both machine and human. This means we need to determine how the service will interact with the calling applications, and through what mechanisms. As in step 3, we define both approaches and testing mechanisms to test these interfaces: what goes in, what should come out, and how quickly.

5. Define how the service is to be tested holistically, using the steps above. This is a very important but often neglected step in which we define how those leveraging the service will test the service within the context of their usage pattern. We must define test information, service invocation, and validity of results, again using black box.

Understanding Your Own Testing Needs

Typically, architectures that leverage both SOA and cloud computing have design patterns that fall into a few major categories:

- Transactional-heavy
- Data-heavy
- Process-heavy

In *transactional-heavy* architectures, the use of transactional services is more apparent than in other architectures. Typically, they are online transaction-processing types of application clusters that use an architecture in which transactional services are leveraged and invoked more than other services.

In *data-heavy* architectures, most of the services employed are data services, or services that broker in information more so than behavior.

In *process-heavy* architectures, the core dynamics of the architecture are driven at the process level. Typically, volatility is the norm in these architectures, and thus the core services are abstracted into a process layer where they can be more easily changed.

Testing Is Important

Testing cloud-based and on-premise services is just a bit more difficult than testing complex distributed systems. To be successful, it requires a great deal of planning and an understanding of the core architecture and interdependencies. In other words, you must test within the context of the architecture, and the two should be linked.

As time goes on, the number of cloud-based remote services that become part of our core systems will increase dramatically. We will surely see new types of domains, such as remote services that leverage remote services, and things will become more complex. The world of SOA using cloud computing is preparing for this complexity with new approaches to architecture, security, and testing, such as identity management, loosely coupled architecture, and better approaches to distributed testing.

CHAPTER 10

Defining Candidate Data, Services, and Processes for the Clouds

When there's snow on the ground, I like to pretend I'm walking on clouds.

—Takayuki Ikkaku, Arisa Hosaka,
and Toshihiro Kawabata
Animal Crossing: Wild World, 2005

Now we're cooking. We have an information, service, process, and governance understanding of our problem domain, and we understand how to approach testing. Now it is time to identify the data, services, and processes that are good candidates for cloud computing. In the next chapter, we move them out there as well as define the end-state architecture and how to extend our SOA out to the clouds.

Keep in mind that we are doing a bit of a distributed computing balancing act now, deploying services, processes, and data on platforms that make the most sense, and we are doing so in the context of SOA. What we are defining here is a mere instance of the architecture, and if it is defined and deployed correctly, we should be able to move our services, processes, and data between on-premise and cloud-based systems without a great deal of difficulty.

The way to get SOA using cloud computing architecture right, right out of the gate, is to identify those services, processes, and data that are good candidates for cloud computing. Once those services are in the clouds, we are likely not to relocate them anytime soon. Moreover, we

179

need to consider all of the issues, such as integration, coupling, security, and risks. This chapter guides you through holistic decisions on how things should be distributed between on-premise and cloud-based platforms that provide the best advantages and value to the core business.

The core objective of this chapter is to provide the basic information needed when looking at architectural components and evaluating their fit for cloud computing. In short, it is all about looking closely at what you have and where you need to be, understanding the trade-off of on-premise and cloud computing, and then drawing the line within the architecture as to what processes, data, and services live where and for what purpose. It is not just about moving services, processes, and data to cloud computing platforms; it is about binding those components into metaprocesses and applications that address any number of business problems.

Where Are the Applications?

Keep in mind that we define services, processes, and data as the basis for applications, with the realization that these services, processes, and data will be bound together to form applications. The reason we address our components this way is that it is much easier to mix and match services, data, and processes among computing resources, whether on-premise or cloud-based, than to move complete applications made up of many services, processes, and data. Providing more granular architectural options allows the architect complete control down to the service, process, and data layers.

When You Are Too Distributed

Your SOA using cloud computing deals with very fine-grained architectural components, including services, processes, and data, so there is the problem of going a bit too crazy. Take the case of a single application that you might scatter services across four cloud computing platforms and perhaps leave a few services on-premise. While this seems like something you would not attempt, going forward there will be many instances where the data may live on an infrastructure-as-a-service provider, such as Amazon EC2, while the user interface lives on a remote Web server, and the core services reside on-premise. This is the world we are moving toward.

However, you could find that your architecture has performance and reliability issues because you leveraged too many platforms to host those services. The problem arises when you consider that the application is dependent on every service functioning in order to continue processing, and thus a single platform failure could stop the entire application from working, depending on how it is designed. In essence, your reliability is really a function of the reliability of all systems, on-premise or cloud-based, that support that application. Consider the number of links in the chain. The more you distribute the application, the more likely you are to have reliability issues. That is the reality of distributed computing.

Furthermore, you should consider performance. It is well known that SOA services that are too finely grained have a tendency to cause performance problems, since each service needs to talk to other services through a single interface. The more services, the more communications occur, and the more the network and the processors get saturated. There are no hard and fast rules around granularity for SOA, or SOA leveraging cloud computing; it is simply a matter of understanding how your architecture will be affected by additional services and understanding the functional need to break down the services into smaller, more fine-grained services.

There are trade-offs, and perhaps you should not go too nuts when decomposing services, from coarse- to fine-grained services, and distributing them across too many systems and platforms, on-premise or in the clouds.

In essence, we identify locations where the services, processes, and data—the architectural components—will reside, and we determine how those components will make up applications. In other words, we break our architecture down to the primitives of services, processes, and data. Then we figure out where to best place them, taking into consideration the business and technical issues we looked at in the last several chapters, and we determine the proper platforms to host those components.

Consider the next several figures, as a way to better understand this process. Figure 10.1 is a starting point. Using the steps and processes covered in the last several chapters, we have a service, process, and data understanding of our problem domain, and we understand what each architectural component does and the interdependencies of each.

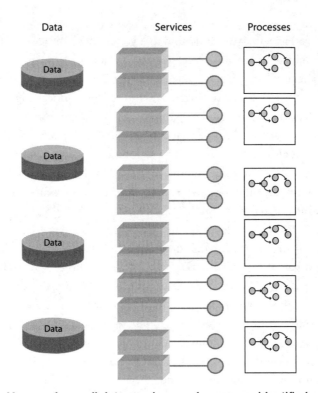

Figure 10.1   Here we have all data, services, and processes identified and detailed.

Figure 10.2 shows the same data, services, and processes that are relocated to cloud computing platforms, in this case, infrastructure-as-a-service, platform-as-a-service, and a single database to database-as-a-service. We now have the architectural components—processes, services, and data—existing across various platforms, both on-premise and cloud computing based.

We chose the right locations for the data, services, and processes, and thus for the applications, on the basis of three factors: the analysis we suggest in this chapter, the business case from Chapter 4, "Making the Business Case for Clouds" and our own IT requirements, such as the need for agility, performance, security, and compliance. Which services, processes, and data should exist? For what reason? Where should they reside? If we are locating them to cloud computing, what type of cloud computing platform should we use? And which cloud computing provider should we choose? There is a lot to think about, and much of it is domain dependent. This book provides some guidance, its better architecture forethought is also required to make the right calls.

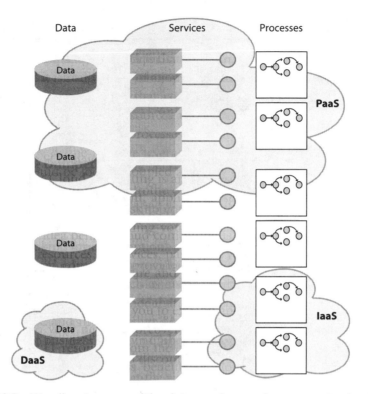

Figure 10.2 We allocate some of the data, services, and processes to cloud computing platforms, where it makes sense to do so. In this example, we use platform-as-a-service (PaaS), infrastructure-as-a-service (IaaS), and database-as-a-service (DaaS). However, your cloud needs are largely dependent on your own business and technology requirements.

Figure 10.3 shows the architecture depicted in Figure 10.2, but this time we defined applications, or bundles of data, processes, and services that can be considered applications or, more accurately, composite applications. These can exist on a single platform, on-premise, or in the clouds, or they can exist between on-premise platforms and the clouds.

The applications are what the business sees out of the architecture, and they are very important to the architecture. Also, keep in mind that applications should share services, processes, and data, thus promoting the benefit of reuse for our SOA using cloud computing. Moreover, the architecture should support the core concept of agility, meaning that it can change through configuration mechanisms and not drive continual redevelopment.

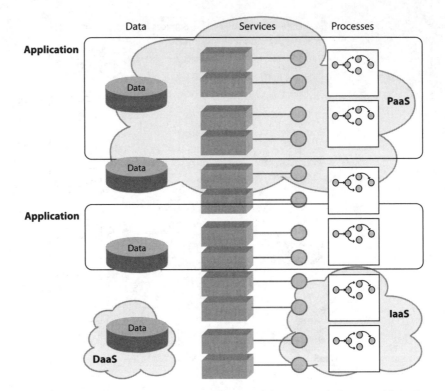

Figure 10.3 Applications are bundles of data, processes, services, and interfaces that form business systems. They can be either on-premise cloud computing–based systems or a hybrid of both. Business users see the architecture through the applications.

If we are going to put this into a process, we must analyze the candidate processes, candidate services, and metadata we defined in the previous steps, and then assign them the proper platform (see Figure 10.4). We discuss the analysis process in the remainder of this chapter, focusing on what to move. In the next chapter, we talk about how to make the move.

When Cloud Computing Fits

There are no hard and fast rules for how to assign a process, data, or service to a cloud computing–based or on-premise platform. It is a matter of look-ing at each component and at the more holistic application, and then analyz-

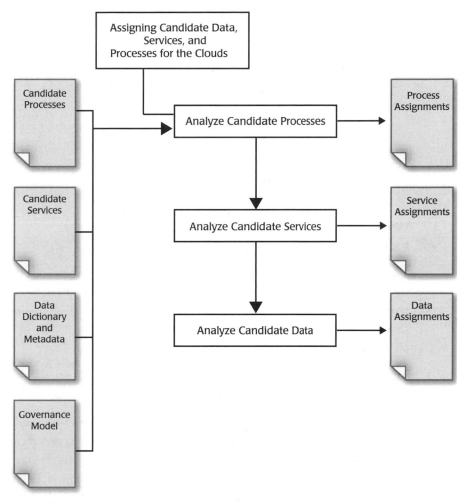

Figure 10.4 Here we need to analyze data, services, and processes, and assign them to an on-premise or a cloud computing–based platform. The inputs are from the artifacts we created in the previous chapters.

ing the attributes and considering the best fit for the architecture and thus the best fit for the business.

However, you can consider some patterns when looking at processes, services, and data and thus make some educated calls as to where to place them. You will find that many are fairly obvious and others require some critical thinking.

Let's look at where cloud computing might be a fit:

- When the processes, applications, and data are largely independent (loosely coupled).
- When the points of integration are well defined.
- When a lower level of security will work just fine.
- When the core internal enterprise architecture is healthy.
- When the browser is the desired user interface.
- When money is tight.
- When the applications and/or services are new.

When the Processes, Applications, and Data Are Largely Independent, or Loosely Coupled

The more the processes, data, and services are coupled, the more dependent they are on each other and the more difficult it is to allow them to be split between cloud and on-premise platforms, or even between cloud computing providers and on-premise systems. The core issue is that if they are coupled and a cloud-hosted process becomes unavailable—for instance, if there is a loss of connectivity—then the lack of that process will halt other processes and services or an entire application. This problem will be more prevalent when processes reside in the cloud.

For processes, services, and data to be good candidates for cloud computing systems, they should leverage a loosely coupled architecture, meaning that the dependencies between services, data, and processes are largely eliminated or reduced. More to the point, loose coupling describes an approach whereby integration interfaces are developed with minimal assumptions between the architectural components that are coupled. This reduces the risk that a change in one architectural component will force a change in another architectural component. A loosely coupled architecture is the core benefit of leveraging SOA. The synergy between SOA and cloud computing exists because cloud computing is simply the extension of your SOA out to the platforms of the clouds.

As you may recall, tight coupling, in the context of architecture, is the binding together of services, processes, and data in such a way that they are dependent on each other, sharing the same methods, interfaces, and, perhaps, data. In essence, coupling is the tight binding of one service, process, or data to the next. As a consequence of this requirement, all tightly coupled services, processes, and data must be extensively changed. Further, as events and circumstances evolve over time, any change to any architectural component demands a corresponding change to the tightly coupled component as well.

When the Points of Integration Are Well Defined

Architectural components placed on cloud computing platforms should have well-defined interfaces to integrate those components back to on-premise components—services, data, or processes or complete applications made up of those components. The architecture should also have the ability to link its components to other cloud-based systems, such as infrastructure-as-a-service, platform-as-a-service, and database-as-a-service. The better the point of integration for an architectural component, the better that component can live in a distributed world.

Anything placed on a cloud computing platform should have the ability to be easily integrated with on-premise or other cloud computing–based systems and thus with well-defined interfaces, such as APIs. Architects and developers can then bind these systems leveraging loosely coupled integration mechanisms, such as Web Services, and allowing them to seamlessly work together to create a holistic architecture that supports the free flow of information along with the ability to invoke services or bind them using processes. If the interfaces are not well defined, then integration is more difficult, perhaps even impossible, so placing them on cloud computing platforms will be less than productive.

When a Lower Level of Security Will Work Just Fine

A lower level of security will work just fine when we are not placing highly sensitive data on cloud computing platforms and thereby putting the business at risk. This does not mean that cloud computing–based systems cannot be secure, leveraging state-of-the-art security approaches, standards, and enabling technology. However, considering sensitivity and compliance issues, some information is not a good fit to exist outside of the firewall.

Some data, such as government secrets, are just too sensitive to be placed on cloud computing platforms because those platforms, even those with a high degree of security, are not wholly controlled by IT. You have to use your own judgment, considering the information and the consequences if it were compromised. If the risk is very high, then it is better to leverage on-premise. If the risks are low, then perhaps a cloud computing platform would work just fine.

Although we know that sensitive data may not be a good fit for cloud computing platforms, you need to carefully consider what constitutes "sensitive data." Many enterprises tend to call all data sensitive, but that is almost never the case. While sales data should be protected and wrapped in a well-thought-out security strategy that encompasses both cloud computing and on-premise systems, is it truly sensitive data? If the sales data somehow leaks, it is unlikely to kill the business.

There is no reason to give up security when leveraging cloud computing. As previously mentioned, a well-thought-out security strategy and security technology will be more than secure for most business systems that reside in the clouds. In many instances, cloud computing systems are more secure than on-premise systems, considering that cloud computing–based systems tend to get special consideration from the security architects because of the concerns about lack of ownership and control. Also, the cloud computing systems are typically new, which means they have incorporated the latest security measures.

Compliance is easier to figure out, since it often means that if you place your data outside of your firewall, you are breaking the law. Or, the data must be handled in a specific way to adhere to a law or regulation. Typically, such regulation protects health information, financial data, corporate governance, and so on. You must understand the compliance issues before selecting processes, data, and services that are to reside in the clouds.

Keep in mind that you need to understand the issues firsthand; do not rely on speculation. In many cases, you will find that everyone assumes the information is not allowed to reside on cloud-based platforms, and yet when you review the actual regulations, that turns out not to be the case. It is common for those in IT to dismiss cloud computing on the basis of assumptions that are not at all true, and they lose out on an opportunity to make their architecture more cost effective.

When the Core Internal Enterprise Architecture Is Healthy

When the core internal enterprise architecture is healthy, you have an existing architecture that is in good working order and lives up to the expectations of the business, and thus you are ready to look at cloud computing. This is a bit of a sidetrack when looking at the architectural components of services, processes, and data as candidates for cloud computing, but it is nonetheless important when you consider that you should not replatform an architecture to or build new applications on cloud computing platforms unless you have healthy enterprise architecture.

Those looking to fix bad enterprise architecture simply by relocating portions of it to cloud computing platforms will find they only make their issues worse. When looking to leverage cloud computing, you should first have your house in good order, meaning that the internal architecture is in a good optimal state. In many instances, architects view cloud computing as a "quick fix" for architectural issues, and it actually makes things more complex and difficult to manage, and it increases the likelihood of business systems failure.

When the Browser Is the Desired User Interface

When the browser is the desired user interface means many cloud computing-based systems, such as infrastructure-as-a-service and platform-as-a-service, leverage browser-based interfaces as the preferred mechanism to interact with a user. These days, most browser-based applications are rich Internet applications (RIAs; see Book Blog) and have the ability to behave and appear native despite running within a browser.

The line between on-premise browser-based applications and cloud-delivered browser-based applications is pretty blurry right now, so there is a lot to think about here. We are simply making the case that if the application lives in a browser, which many already do, then cloud computing has some additional benefits.

Cloud computing applications leverage Web-based interfaces because they are serving up applications over the Internet that support platform independence by leveraging the browser as the common denominator. However, in some cases, end users want to leverage the native user interfaces, such as Windows or Mac, and do not want to leverage a browser. With the advent of RIA and the pervasive use of the browser as the common user interface, native user interfaces are not as likely to be widely available in the clouds.

RIA, SOA, and Cloud Computing

A rich client, or an RIA, is a small piece of software that runs on the client to leverage and aggregate back-end services, allowing them to appear as a single, unified, native application. A new interface is needed as both developers and end users begin to understand the limitations of traditional Web-based interfaces, which are the current interfaces of choice for many distributed applications.

However, RIA is everywhere today. It is the primary interface leveraged by Google and many other on-demand office automation systems. By leveraging RIAs, it can offer a dynamic and reactive user interface that appears to be native. No longer must we deal with the traditional browser interfaces where Web pages are constantly being sent to and from the server and the user deals more often with an hourglass than a live application.

Web interfaces in wide use within enterprises were never really designed to support true interactive applications. The Web was built as a content provider, serving up documents and not dynamic application services. If you think about it, you are reloading document after document to simulate an interactive application and always have to go to the back-end Web server to request new content. Very little occurs at the client.

As the Web became popular and we looked to support business applications within the enterprise using the Web interface, we began to create new mechanisms to deliver dynamic content, including dynamic HTTP/HTML pushers (e.g., Common Gateway Interface, Apache Server Application Programming Interface, Internet Server Application Programming Interface) and new browsers that supported complex dynamic behavior. We are at such an advanced state today that entire enterprises run most of their relevant business applications using Web interfaces.

However, with the advent of software-as-a-service (aka, application-as-a-service), the Web 2.0, and now cloud computing, there is a need to leverage dynamic behavior within the interfaces. Traditional browsers fall way short. Their get/push model for driving interfaces is not as well suited to support dynamic applications, which are, at their essence, remote functions better suited for more visually rich types of interfaces, such as more traditional GUI client/server interfaces that were popular a few years ago.

RIAs are not a revolution but an evolution of technology, including Asynchronous JavaScript and XML (AJAX). Today we look to leverage dynamic behavior and deliver that experience directly to the end user, aggregating

Web Services within an interface that appears as much as possible like a native application.

What is AJAX?

Ajax, sometimes written as AJAX . . . is a group of interrelated Web development techniques used to create interactive Web applications or rich Internet applications. Ajax is said to be a client-side specification, for the creation of Web pages, Web sites, or Web applications. With Ajax, Web applications can retrieve data from the server asynchronously in the background without interfering with the display and behavior of the existing page.[1]

RIAs that employ AJAX provide capabilities that thin clients cannot provide, including windowing features and data navigation controls such as buttons, check boxes, radio buttons, toggles. and palettes. They can also integrate content, communications, and platform-independent application interfaces for distribution through SOAs and cloud computing. RIA using AJAX becomes a Web Services/SOA terminal of sorts, allowing applications to communicate and even execute on one another within a distributed environment (see Figure 10.5).

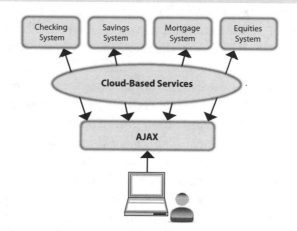

Figure 10.5 Using AJAX and RIA, we can create composite RIAs by leveraging many back-end services and data on-premise or from cloud computing platforms.

continued

---

1. http://en.wikipedia.org/wiki/AJAX.

This is great news for those of us who develop Web Services or implement SOA on-premise or via cloud computing. With the use of RIAs, suddenly those services have a much higher value. You can mix and match services within a rich client to create some very valuable applications.

Rich clients give us the ability to view applications that look and act like native client programs even though they run remotely. That is a step in the right direction—and the reason RIA is so important to SOA and cloud computing.

When Money Is Tight

Cloud computing is an alternative to consider seriously when cost savings is an issue. As we covered in Chapter 4, cloud computing is typically (but not always) less expensive. If budgets are tight, cloud computing may be the best option, and we stress *may*. There are a few rules of thumb here.

First, new companies (startups) and their data, services, and processes are typically the best fit for cloud computing given that their applications are new (we cover this next) and that they need to operate with the least possible amount of overhead. Therefore, the requirement for cheap and new turns most new companies toward cloud computing. I suspect as they grow that the use of cloud computing resources for their IT infrastructure will give them a huge advantage in the marketplace when looking at efficiencies relative to their larger and older competitors.

Second, existing companies looking to leverage cloud computing need to carefully consider the true cost advantage of doing so. A typical movement to the cloud will be an application prototype that is built on an infrastructure-as-a-service or platform-as-a-service cloud, with the battle cry of "cost reduction." And it seems logical that an application infrastructure that costs $10 a day is better than an on-premise infrastructure that costs $100 a day. However, when you consider all of the costs, including integration, risk, security, management, and all the things we discussed in Chapter 4, the cost savings are somewhat diluted if not eliminated.

Avoiding "Hype Mistakes" around Cloud Computing

Cloud computing is well-hyped technology; there is no getting around this fact. Those moving toward cloud computing, either by building new services, processes, and databases on cloud-based platforms or, more likely, by relocating entire systems to cloud-based platforms, could being doing so because of the hype and the buzz around cloud computing. You can make a huge mistake here.

At issue is that the temptation to improve a résumé or just to play with new toys could influence many in IT more than the goal to make their IT infrastructure more cost effective. Many cloud computing projects are really a reaction to the hype more than a clear business need. While this is to be expected during any "hype cycle," the end result is on-premise pegs in cloud holes, raising issues around the longevity of those systems considering that they are not good candidates for cloud computing at the end of the day.

How do you avoid hype mistakes? Make sure that the gating factor of the business case is always in place and that there is a clear business benefit from moving toward cloud computing. It is also a good idea to have an independent reviewer or committee participate in the process to objectively review the fit with cloud computing (use sparingly and leverage people without agendas). If these governance processes are not put in place, I suspect that we will have many cloud computing misfits.

The key is that you find the true costs—all of the costs associated with building and maintaining the processes, services, and data you are looking to place in the clouds. I suspect that many components that are moved out to cloud platforms under the notion of cost reduction will not be as cost effective as most might expect. Do your business case around each service, data, process, and application.

When the Applications and/or Services Are New

New applications, including services, processes, and data, are almost always a much better fit for cloud computing than are legacy applications. There are a few core reasons that new applications are a better fit.

First, legacy applications (including services, processes, and data) typically have to go through a partial or total rewrite in order to successfully exist on cloud computing platforms. While many existing systems are in need of a rewrite, the reality is that having to redesign, rewrite, and redeploy services, data, and processes for cloud-based platforms substantially increases the risk and the cost. A move to the clouds therefore needs to be carefully cost justified.

Second, distributed systems are much happier if they are designed from the ground up as distributed systems. Many attempt to port existing systems to cloud platforms, patching what needs to be patched around moving a monolithic and centralized system to a cloud-based platform. In order to take full advantage, it should be broken down to the core services, data, and processes, and built up again as a true distributed system that can leverage a loosely coupled architecture.

Finally, if it ain't broke, don't fix it. Many existing systems provide core value to the business, and while they are costly to operate, the risk of moving these core systems to new platforms may outweigh any cost benefit obtained through the use of cloud computing. We have all seen projects with the title "modernization" that have ended in total failure and negatively impacted the business.

Jumping to the Clouds

As you can see, there are no hard and fast rules governing what services, processes, and data should reside in the cloud. It is a matter of understanding your existing IT resources, the existing architecture, and then, through careful analysis, figuring out which services, processes, and data should be cloud-based and which should remain on-premise.

Mistakes that are typically made during this process involve a misinterpretation of what cloud computing–based providers can actually bring to the party. You understand cloud computing largely through the hyperbole, which is driven largely by the cloud computing providers, and you need to focus on what works and on best practices rather than on what is cool and hot. There is a huge difference.

Another concept to keep in mind is that your architecture should remain independent of the technology whenever possible. Technology will constantly change, but the architecture should remain relatively stable. Do not bind your architecture to any technology or cloud computing provider.

Finally, if you are unsure about the fit for cloud computing, it is a good idea to create a proof-of-concept prototype that provides additional insight. The great thing about cloud computing providers is that you can quickly create a prototype without a major infrastructure investment. The data points gathered for this type of effort are invaluable.

In the next chapter, we look at platform issues, including how to pick the right cloud categories and cloud providers that are right for your architecture, and also how to actually make the move. At this point, we have picked the architectural components that should reside in the cloud, and that unto itself is a major step forward as we look to benefit from extending our SOAs to the clouds.

CHAPTER 11

Making the Move to Cloud Computing

*The important work of moving the world forward
does not wait to be done by perfect men.*

—George Eliot (1819–1880)

Okay, now we have a data-, services-, and process-level understanding of our problem domain. We know how to test it, and we know how we are going to govern it. In Chapter 10, "Defining Candidate Data, Services, and Processes for the Clouds," we figured out which processes, services, and data should reside on-premise and which should be cloud-based. Now we need to implement our final physical architecture, meaning we pick the proper platforms, test those platforms so that we know they meet our requirements, and move and/or create the processes, services, and data on the clouds.

There are a few things to remember here. First, this is just a physical instance of our architecture. The technology will change, but our architecture should remain fairly stable. This is more so the case with cloud computing, since changing cloud computing providers is much easier and less costly than changing on-premise systems.

Second, we select the technology or cloud computing provider during this final step. We reserved this decision until now because we wanted to remain objective up to this point to consider the valuable information that came to light during the processes we followed in the last several chapters. If we get into this with the technology in mind, we are likely to skew the architecture toward that technology, which could be the wrong choice.

Finally, the number of hardware, software, and cloud computing providers leveraged will be many or few, depending on the needs of the architecture. No matter the numbers, our solution simply needs to be the appropriate one. Some target architectural instances will be complex, some simplistic, depending on the needs of the business and what we determined in the last several steps outlined in this book.

In this chapter, we focus on the cloud computing part of the architecture, including all on-premise and cloud computing–based systems. We are, as you may recall, simply extending our SOA to the platform of the clouds. We must deal with all on-premise hardware and software issues as well, including leveraging existing systems, creating new systems and services, adding new technology and governance, incorporating security, and so on.

Also, this chapter introduces the concept of the private cloud, which we covered briefly in Chapter 1, "Where We Are, How We Got Here, and How to Fix It." Private clouds are virtualized hardware and software resources that exist within the firewall, within the data center, providing cloud computing–like characteristics around the ability to better utilize hardware and software resources within the enterprise. This is also an architectural option.

Selecting Platforms

As you can see in Figure 11.1, there are many patterns, or categories, in the world of cloud computing that you can leverage to meet the needs of your architecture. Some, such as security-as-a-service and testing-as-a-service, solve specific problems, and others, such as platform-as-a-service and infrastructure-as-a-service, provide complete platforms. They all have trade-offs and different problems that each solves. However, you must consider them all in light of your architecture.

While we covered the characteristics of these cloud computing providers in Chapter 3, "Defining the Clouds for the Enterprise," it is a good idea to look at how they can fit into our architecture here, starting first with granularity of the providers. The categories are

- Storage-as-a-service
- Database-as-a-service
- Information-as-a-service

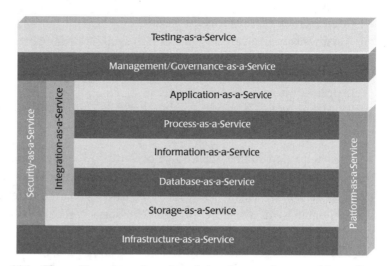

Figure 11.1 The patterns or categories of cloud computing providers allow you to leverage a discrete set of services within your architecture.

- Process-as-a-service
- Application-as-a-service
- Platform-as-a-service
- Integration-as-a-service
- Security-as-a-service
- Management/governance-as-a-service
- Testing-as-a-service
- Infrastructure-as-a-service

We can further break them down into fine-grained solutions, or those providers who solve very specific problems that alone cannot be considered a platform, and coarse-grained providers, or those who unto themselves are a complete platform.

Fine-Grained

1. Storage-as-a-service
2. Database-as-a-service
3. Information-as-a-service
4. Process-as-a-service
5. Integration-as-a-service
6. Security-as-a-service

7. Management/governance-as-a-service
8. Testing-as-a-service

Coarse-Grained

9. Application-as-a-service
10. Platform-as-a-service
11. Infrastructure-as-a-service

It is helpful to do this breakdown because one coarse-grained cloud computing provider can actually be made up of many fine-grained resources. For example, a single platform-as-as-service provider could offer storage-as-a-service, database-as-a-service, process-as-a-service, security-as-a-service, and testing-as-a-service.

However, while it may seem easier to leverage a coarse-grained cloud computing solution because it provides many fine-grained resources, the requirements of your architecture may dictate a finer-grained solution. You may find that selecting many fine-grained cloud computing solutions is a much better fit for your architecture when considering your requirements and/or the ability to mesh effectively with the on-premise portion of the architecture.

Also, we need to look at the capabilities of each platform that hosts the services, processes, and information we defined and refined in the previous chapters. The candidate cloud computing provider categories are, by architectural component,

Processes
- Application-as-a-service
- Platform-as-a-service
- Infrastructure-as-a-service
- Process-as-a-service
- Integration-as-a-service

Data
- Application-as-a-service
- Platform-as-a-service
- Infrastructure-as-a-service
- Storage-as-a-service
- Database-as-a-service
- Information-as-a-service

Services

- Application-as-a-service
- Platform-as-a-service
- Infrastructure-as-a-service
- Information-as-a-service

To make this point clearer, here are a few examples of physical instances of architecture. We first selected categories of cloud computing providers, and then we selected the providers (Example 11.1).

Example 11.1

Processes:
　　　　Process-as-a-service
　　　　　　Appian Anywhere

Data:
　　　　Infrastructure-as-a-service
　　　　　　Amazon EC2
　　　　Database-as-a-service
　　　　　　Amazon Simple DB

Services:
　　　　Infrastructure-as-a-service
　　　　　　Amazon EC2

For instance, we may store our data within Amazon Simple DB as well as on the Amazon EC2 platforms. Then, we might build and/or host the services on the Amazon EC2 platform, say, using an application server they provide on-demand within that platform. Finally, we could leverage Appian Anywhere as the platform where those processes live. Keep in mind that the processes are connected to the services, and the services are connected to the data, as we described in earlier chapters. We are just selecting the target platforms here.

This solution could become more complex by leveraging more cloud computing providers (Example 11.2).

Example 11.2

Processes:
　　　　Process-as-a-service
　　　　　　Appian Anywhere
　　　　Application-as-a-service
　　　　　　Salesforce.com

Data:
> Infrastructure-as-a-service
>> 3Tera Cloudware
>> Amazon EC2
>
> Database-as-a-service
>> Amazon Simple DB

Services:
> Infrastructure-as-a-service
>> Amazon EC2
>> 3Tera Cloudware
>
> Application-as-a-service
>> Salesforce.com
>
> Platform-as-a-service
>> Force.com

Or, as in Example 11.3, it could become a bit less complex by leveraging a single infrastructure-as-a-service cloud computing provider.

Example 11.3

Processes:
> Process-as-a-service
>> Amazon EC2

Data:
> Infrastructure-as-a-service
>> Amazon EC2

Services:
> Infrastructure-as-a-service
>> Amazon EC2

We must also consider the other core components of the architecture, including security and governance, which can be deployed as on-premise or cloud-based, depending on our needs. Testing also can be delivered as a service or be on-premise as well.

The purpose of this exercise is to illustrate the number of architectural options we have, and how we can mix and match them, to form our final architecture using as many or as few as needed to address the requirements of the architecture and the business.

The Process of Moving to the Clouds

Figure 11.2 depicts the high-level process we can leverage to find the right cloud computing category or categories and the right cloud computing provider or providers to move the processes, services, and data we selected as good cloud computing candidates.

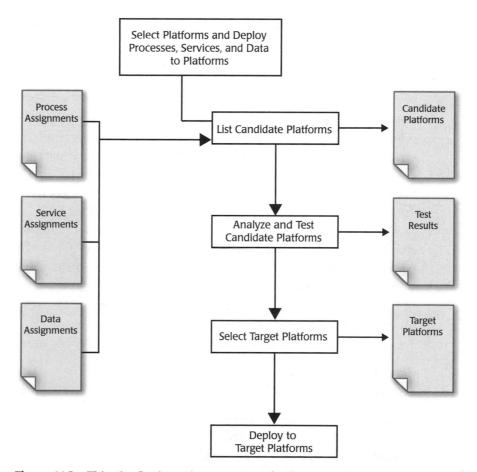

Figure 11.2 This, the final step in our process, is all about taking the process, service, and data requirements and mapping them to the right technology.

The core steps are as follows:

- List candidate platforms.
- Analyze and test candidate platforms.
- Select target platforms.
- Deploy to target platforms.

Let's look at each step in more detail.

List Candidate Platforms

Listing candidate platforms is pretty simple considering the information presented earlier. You need to list any and all cloud computing platforms that may be a fit for your to-be architecture. This requires that you understand what solutions are available, their categories, and what they do.

There are no hard and fast rules for defining a cloud computing solution. Thus, many software providers, whether they have a true cloud computing solution or not, have a tendency to say they do. For example, a few software vendors claim that since their software can be downloaded over the Web to an on-premise computing system, they are an on-demand or cloud computing platform. They are not. Therefore, this step can be a bit about separating the wheat from the chaff, more so than just tossing together a list.

We do not list cloud computing providers in this book, since that world changes monthly, with providers constantly being added, deleted, or combined. Mastery of SOA using cloud computing is as much about keeping up with the market space as it is about understanding what the vendors provide. In support of this process, you can visit the book's Web site to see an updated list of vendors and their categories.

In choosing your candidates, you must answer two key questions:

1. What categories do you need?
2. Which cloud computing providers in these categories should we consider?

The categories you leverage depend on the final logical architecture and the requirements you identified through this process. We can make some generalizations, though, including the fundamental layers you require and what to look for within each layer (see Figure 11.3):

- Storage
- Database

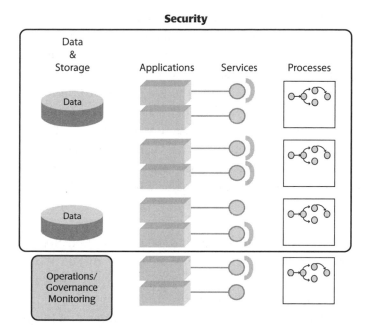

Figure 11.3 The core architecture requires you to find places for storage, data, operations, governance, security, services, and processes.

- Processes
- Services
- Security
- Governance
- Management

Storage is the category that supports part or all of the architecture in storing, sharing, and managing file systems. You typically leverage storage-as-a-service for this, either from a cloud computing provider that only provides storage-as-a-service, or as part of an infrastructure-as-a-service cloud computing provider.

Things you need to look out for here are capacity and performance. Capacity is your ability to scale your storage needs to support your architecture. Performance is your ability to move files to and from the cloud computing service at a speed that supports the business. Performance problems are the most likely issue here, so make sure you do your testing.

Database and database-as-a-service is the storage and retrieval of data using a platform-as-a-service, database-as-a-service, or infrastructure-as-a-service. Things you need to consider here include the ability for the cloud-delivered database to support the features and functions you may require for your architecture, including the use of stored procedures and triggers, the function of the API, adherence to standards, and performance.

Within the case of infrastructure-as-a-service, cloud computing providers typically allow you to leverage name brand databases, such as Oracle or MySQL. However, the database-as-a-service providers typically use a home-grown rather than brand-name database, and they tend to be more proprietary in nature.

Performance comes into play here as well. Most on-premise and traditional applications are data I/O bound, so you will find that similar performance problems may exist here. Consider the overhead of I/O on a multitenant platform and the latency that can occur when you send large amounts of data to and from your enterprise to the cloud computing provider and back again over the Internet. This could also make a case for placing the database closer to the processes and services that leverage that database, which is a core tenet of architecture when you consider performance and the reliability of databases.

Always Check on the Frequency of Outages

For all of this to work, reliability is a core requirement of your cloud computing provider. As you select cloud computing providers for your to-be architecture, make sure to look at the reliability of each provider. Typically, this means looking at the number of outages they experienced over a 2-year period. Also, look at how they support failover and other recovery operations when events such as network, hardware, and software failures occur.

While many of these outages make the IT press, the lesser known cloud computing providers often go unnoticed when outages occur. Make sure to call a few references—both those the vendor provides and perhaps a few they do not—and ask about the frequency of outages. Also, if the cloud computing provider is good, it should have a record of outages, why they occurred, and what they are doing to prevent such outages in the future.

Processes can exist on process-as-a-service, platform-as-a-service, application-as-a-service, and infrastructure-as-a-service providers, for the most part. You need to consider a few issues here.

When using process-as-a-service providers, keep in mind that processes are all they do. You must therefore bind the other architectural components (typically services and data) to those processes. The data and service assets exist either within on-premise systems or with other cloud computing providers, so you must make sure that integration occurs and is reliable.

Application-as-a-service providers typically do not provide a platform for you to create your own processes but allow you to leverage prebuilt processes on their platform. This is handy because, for instance, you need not create a custom fulfillment process for your business—you can just leverage theirs. However, as with the process-as-a-service, the processes are isolated and thus must be linked back with other on-premise and cloud computing–delivered systems that are part of the architecture.

When considering infrastructure-as-a-service providers and platform-as-a-service providers, you are typically dealing with platforms that provide the "complete stack," including storage, database, processes, applications, services, development, testing, and more. These processes are just a component of those platforms. It may seem tempting to leverage "complete stack" providers, since they do indeed provide one-stop shopping for cloud computing. However, you will have to make trade-offs: You might love the application development features of one platform-as-a-service provider but hate the way its product manages processes or find that its process engine is sluggish. In many cases, it may be better to leverage other cloud computing providers or even on-premise software to address processes, trading simplicity for complexity but leveraging a process engine that is the right fit for the architecture.

Services (e.g., Web Services), generally speaking, can live on most cloud computing platforms. However, only a few (including platform-as-a-service, process-as-a-service, and infrastructure-as-a-service) provide the capabilities to create and host services through which application-as-a-service and information-as-a-service provide access to their hosted prebuilt services, which you can use but cannot change.

The most common issue here is performance. Services such as Web Services (whether using REST or SOAP) tend to cause performance problems if the platform hosting the service cannot provide enough computing resources, or if there are too many services and they saturate the platform and the network. Again, you need to test for performance by actually using the services, and adjust your platform, the number of services you leverage, and the way those services are designed to optimize the performance of your architecture.

Security is not a platform or a piece of software that exists on-premise or on cloud computing platforms. If done right, it should be systemic to the holistic architecture, no matter how much of it is on-premise or cloud computing–delivered. You address security by creating a strategy and a model to secure your architecture based on the requirements you identified. Then you select the proper approach and supporting enabling technology. Security typically centers on identity management and the standards that support identity management.

With the increasing interest in identity management, in support of more complex and distributed architectures such as SOA and SOA using cloud computing, the need for standards to better define this space has arisen. These standards all aim to bind together identity management systems within all organizations into a unified whole, allowing for everyone to be known to everyone else, securely.

Why do we need identity management? It is a fact that services are not for internal use anymore, as is the case when leveraging cloud computing. Those who leverage services (consumers) and those who produce services (providers) must be known to each other; otherwise, we risk invoking malicious or incorrect behavior, which could cost us dearly. This is clearly the case with cloud computing that leverages services.

Governance brings its own set of issues when considering architecture and cloud computing. While there are governance systems that are cloud delivered, and they work well for some types of architecture, governance systems that implement, manage, and enforce policies are runtime in nature and are typically on-premise.

Issues to look out for here again include performance, since, in some instances, executing policies could cause latency issues. Also important is the governance solution's ability to govern resources, which are typically cloud-delivered services. This means having the ability to track remote services within the governance technology's repository as well as to monitor those services during runtime.

Management of a widely distributed and complex architecture, such as SOA using cloud computing, requires a management technology that can see both on-premise systems, which most do, and cloud computing–based systems, which only a few do well. Moreover, you should check whether the cloud provider has an interface on their software that allows management technology to talk to it.

The core idea is to provide a management platform that sees all on-premise and cloud computing–based systems at the "working or not working" level, at the very least, meaning we can see whether a system is down and how that status will affect other systems in the architecture. However, it is preferable to have a management system that can see systems such as services, processes, data, storage at more granular levels, which makes it much easier to diagnose issues and spot troubles before they happen.

Management and governance are clearly linked and have very similar patterns.

Analyze and Test Candidate Platforms

Once you select the candidate cloud computing platforms, you need to make sure they live up to the requirements we established. You do this through some deep dives into each candidate platform you selected and then through testing.

We covered testing extensively in Chapter 9, "Testing from SOA to the Clouds," so we do not go too deep into it here. However, this testing is a bit different in that you are actually testing the generic capabilities of the cloud computing platform. Specifically, you look at how that cloud computing platform will support the requirements of the architectural components, including services, data, and processes, but you are not yet deploying on those platforms. They could be the wrong choices, which is why we do the testing.

The only thing to add from Chapter 9 is the use of performance modeling and performance testing. Modeling creates a simulation of how the system should perform under different types of loads, typically light, medium, and heavy. Performance testing determines how the architecture performs under stress. It involves modeling the architecture, including how the information will flow and the services will be invoked, and how flow and invocation affect the different computing resources, both on-premise and cloud-based. You should have a general idea as to what performance you can expect from the cloud computing platforms and how things such as decreasing processing power or expanding bandwidth should affect overall performance.

While proving the performance models, you should leverage performance testing, determining how well and how fast the holistic architecture, both on-premise and cloud-based, will support the business. Moreover, measure how the system performs during an ever-increasing storage, database, process, and service-processing load. If they do not perform well, find out where the bottlenecks are: in the network? the database? services? If necessary, work with the cloud provider to correct them.

Select Target Platforms

Once we go through all of the analysis, including a service-, process-, and data-level understanding of our problem domain, and have considered both security and governance, compiled a list of candidate systems, and completed the validation testing, it is time to pick the cloud computing platforms.

This step is pretty easy considering that any issue around the platform's ability to meet the requirements of the architecture, and thus the business, should be well known and understood by now. Also, keep in mind that it is more likely that the final selection of the suite of target cloud computing platforms is very different from what you first envisioned, but if you did your homework and followed each step in this book, they should be the proper platforms for your architecture.

Also worth mentioning is the ease of switching, or should we say, the relative ease of switching, from one cloud computing platform to another if for some reason you make the wrong call, or more likely, if some business event occurs with the cloud computing platform, such as the cloud computing provider going out of business or a merger or acquisition changes or removes that platform. Of course, this depends on the cloud computing provider you selected, its use of standards, and your ability to find another provider that offers similar characteristics and features.

The business issues are more important if you are looking to create an SOA using cloud computing, since that scenario depends entirely on the cloud provider to stay in business and keep up and running. You need to carefully consider

- The viability of the provider and the likelihood that it will provide ongoing support for your cloud computing platforms.
- The provider's ability to recover from hardware, software, and network failures, dynamically and with minimum downtime.

- The service-level agreements, or SLAs, and a meeting of the minds between you and the cloud computing provider as to what service levels need to be supported for your architecture.
- A complete understanding of the policies of the cloud computing provider and what denotes a violation. In some instances, cloud computing providers have, without notice, canceled accounts due to policy violations.

Deploy to Target Platforms

This is the "just do it" step, meaning that we actually port code; migrate data; create new services, processes, and databases; and test and validate that all services, databases, and processes are working correctly and as defined, using the steps in this book.

The approach you should leverage here should be focused on migration and development over time, not a "big bang approach." You should select which components of the architecture should move to or be created on the cloud computing platforms, going from the most important to the least.

As you move these architectural components to the cloud computing platforms, make sure they are functioning correctly and have been properly tested before moving on to the next architectural component. While the pressure may be on to make "the big switch," the reality is that this evolutionary approach prevents problems and does not overwhelm those who deploy services, data, and processes to the cloud computing platforms. Also, this approach provides the value of learn-as-you-go, meaning that your knowledge of how to make cloud computing platforms work for your architecture will increase significantly as we move through this process.

Where Social Networking Fits with Cloud Computing

Opinions on social networking vary widely, from "No way, it's too risky" to "It's a way of life; you might as well learn to leverage it for productivity." Social networking has already been lumped in with cloud computing, so it is a good idea to consider its value and risks. How will you integrate social networking within your SOA using cloud computing architecture? Now is a good time to form a set of policies.

continued

It does not matter whether you understand the differences between MySpace and Facebook. Most of the people who work in your enterprises, IT or not, leverage some sort of social networking system, and most look at it at least once a day during work hours. Assuming you could put your foot down and declare this stuff against policy, most employees would find that a bit too Big Brother–ish and would find a way to do it anyway, perhaps on their cell phones or PDAs. Social networking in the workplace is a fact of life you must deal with, and perhaps it could be another point of value that comes down from the clouds.

To figure out the enterprise opportunities or risks involved with social networking, you first must define the reasons that people leverage social networking:

- To communicate, both passively and actively, in an ongoing manner and through various mediums, with people in whom they are interested—usually with friends and family, but in some cases, the activity is all work related. Typically, it's a mixture of both.
- To learn more about areas of interest. For example, LinkedIn groups, such as SOA, Web 2.0, and enterprise architecture.
- To leverage social networking within the context of the SOA using cloud computing architecture, such as allowing core enterprise systems, on-premise or cloud-based, to exchange information. For instance, social networking can be used to view a customer's Facebook friends list to find new leads, and thus new business opportunities, by integrating Facebook with your sales force management system.

There are risks involved in online social networking, however. People can (and do) lose their jobs because of a posting on a social networking site that put their company at risk. People can be (and have been) publically embarrassed by posting pictures, videos, or other information they thought would be, uhm, private. Also, there are many cases of criminal activity using social networking as a mechanism to commit a crime.

Here is the gist of it. Social networking, in one form or another, is always going to be around. So if you are doing enterprise IT, including cloud computing, you might as well accept it but learn how to govern through education, policies, and perhaps some technology. While there are risks, there are also opportunities, such as the ability to leverage information gathered by social networking sites to enhance marketing and sales, and by integrating those systems with your core business systems, both on-premise and cloud-based.

Make sure to define to all employees when and where it is appropriate to leverage social networking within the workplace. Try not to be too restrictive, but instead inform them of what is a good social networking practice and what is unacceptable. You will find that 99% of those who already leverage social networking are already using their heads.

Keep in mind that leads are being developed, sales made, and customers supported using social networking systems. Not surprisingly, the correct use of social networking can have a very positive effect on the bottom line, especially considering the access to valuable information that these social networking sites provide and the ability to leverage that information to provide better business intelligence to support the core business systems. You may also find that employee-to-employee communication improves using social networking systems, internal or public.

Make sure to work with your legal department to define written policies for social networking, and make sure all employees are aware of and committed to adhering to these policies. The idea is to cover the company in case someone does something stupid. Again, you are mitigating the risk, not eliminating it.

Finally, monitor the use of social networking sites with standard Web governance technology, including logging and trending. This is not to catch a particular person who is leveraging social networking but to determine the patterns of use over time. Also, if particular sites do become a problem, you can shut them off.

What about Private Clouds?

Until now, we have yet to hit on the notion of private clouds, beyond our introduction in Chapter 1. It is important that we dive a bit deeper into the concept here as an architectural option for our SOA using cloud computing while we select platforms for deployment.

Private clouds are cloud computing–like infrastructures that leverage virtualization and exist within private data centers. The core notion is that cloud computing is a great approach to optimize the use of hardware and software, and we can obtain the same value by doing the same trick within our data center using virtualized resources, or private clouds. Most computing resources, such as database servers, application servers, and governance servers, are underutilized, typically running at only 5% of their capacity at any given time (based on my experience and observations).

A private cloud, or more exactly, the use of virtualization software such as VMWare, gives you the ability to address many physical servers as one virtual server and thus to leverage the processing power of all computing resources as if they were a single resource. You can optimize the use of all hardware and software resources more so than if they were bound to a particular hardware and software platform. The virtualization software can allocate the process load between all available servers, which improves the utilization of each computing resource.

The end result is that you can support more data, services, and processes on a fewer number of servers, and this virtualization mechanism reduces costs. This approach is called *private clouds* because it features many of the same benefits of cloud computing, including the ability to reduce costs.

Enterprises are interested in private clouds because, in many instances, they cannot host their data outside of their firewalls due to privacy and legal issues, but they want to take advantage of the cloud computing architecture. Many of them want to remain in control of their systems and information and have already invested in hardware and software, the cost of which cannot be recovered.

Again, private clouds are basically virtualized platforms, and all of the issues that virtualization has attempted to resolve in past years is applicable here. The patterns of virtualized platforms and the patterns of some cloud computing platforms, such as infrastructure-as-a-service, are almost identical other than the location of processing and provisioning. Where public clouds are for anyone who can sign up, and in many instances the cloud users are not verified, private clouds allow only authorized persons, or internal users, to provision themselves on the private clouds.

Many view this utilization of virtualization systems as simply jumping on the bandwagon to ride the cloud computing wave. However, it is the reality of the forthcoming modernization of the enterprise: the need to do much more with much less and to get smarter with sharing resources, both on-premise and remote. While cloud computing will clearly drive some aspects of modern enterprise architecture, the ability to create similar value within existing and paid-for data centers is a viable architectural option and should be considered in the mix.

New "Cloudy" Platforms

The activities outlined in this chapter represent some of the most fun you will have around cloud computing: actually moving systems to the clouds and making those systems work for the business. It is "doing" rather than planning or analyzing, but it is also the trickiest of all the activities we have outlined, and it carries the most risk.

In addition, unless you are reading this book well into the future, you know that the cloud computing platforms are a bit of a moving target, meaning that as the hype and the market heat up, new providers will appear weekly, and existing providers will pack in as much functionality as they can to capture the market.

Cloud computing platforms are easily changed, since they do not require the distribution of software to enterprises, and change will be an ongoing activity: constant upgrades, bug fixes, and other changes to the platform. Hopefully, these changes will move the overall system in better directions and not break your architectural components that exist on these platforms—they will be backward compatible.

What seems like an unnatural act today, as you relocate and create architectural components on cloud computing platforms, will seem second nature as time progresses. Clearly, as we move many of our services, processes, and data out to the clouds, clouds will become a major component of enterprise architecture and SOA.

SOA using cloud computing is the best architectural approach, as you have seen throughout the book. SOA using cloud computing provides the ability to address computing resources using the best possible configuration, and it matters not where those computing resources reside. We continue to extend them to the clouds, and more clouds will surely appear.

CHAPTER 12

Moving Onward

I never think of the future—it comes soon enough.
—Albert Einstein (1879–1955)

It is time to look into the future of SOA using cloud computing. This is not one of those "predictions" chapters. In an FAQ format, we talk about the obvious trends as well as some last-minute advice that you may need as you push your SOA out into the clouds.

Keep in mind that cloud computing will be a quick-moving concept for the next several years. New issues will arise as we learn more, and new opportunities to do cloud computing better and to leverage new and emerging cloud computing resources will present themselves. It is important to keep close track of the cloud computing space as it evolves. Also make sure to monitor Web sites for this book, including the supporting blog, to keep your finger on the pulse of cloud computing and for additional updates on the convergence of SOA and cloud computing.

Q: In the future, will we find most of our core services, processes, and data relocated to cloud computing platforms?

A: Probably not. While cloud computing is a great fit for some applications and/or other architectural components, it typically will not be a fit for all. There will always be some data, services, processes, and complete applications that you want to keep within your firewall for a number of reasons, including compliance, privacy, fear, control, and cost.

However, like anything in the world of computing, nothing is written in stone. Many companies write their own commodity services. If all of those services could be pushed out to the clouds and the companies provided on-premise only those services they think are to their competitive advantage, there would be a whole lot of stuff relocated to the cloud.

Compliance means that it is just plain illegal to place certain architectural components, typically data, outside of the firewall. You should check on the applicable legal requirements because they are typically not well understood. However, there are laws forbidding specific data to exist outside of the firewall or outside of the country. Usually, you find these regulations in the worlds of finance and health care, but they can exist in all business verticals.

Privacy means that, either through policy or demand from those whom the data represents, you cannot place certain personal or sensitive data out on cloud platforms because of the possibility that the data could be compromised. These issues are typically more paranoia than reality, but in some instances, privacy concerns will trump cloud computing. Keep in mind that this is often a people issue, not a technology issue. There is no reason you cannot keep data private on cloud computing platforms if you take the appropriate precautions (see the discussion of security later in this chapter).

Fear means that people are just plain afraid of cloud computing and view it as something that will lead to massive failure of core enterprise systems: that data will be lost, data will be compromised, or data will fall victim to any other evil. The root of the fear is that systems not under your direct control will crash, and you will be unable to do anything about it. This is clearly a people issue, again, and you must teach those who fear cloud computing about its benefits, listen carefully to their concerns, and address their fears directly.

Control means that people view their role within IT as significant and that they should continue to control all architectural assets. They feel everything should remain within the data center. These are the "need to hug my server" crowd, and this is another people issue. Some people refuse to allow cloud computing because of control issues, no matter what business benefits you present to them.

Cost means there are some applications and architectural components (services, processes, and data) that simply make no sense to extend to cloud computing because there are no direct cost savings or other business benefits. While you can make a business case for some applications, cloud computing is almost never cost effective or a good technical fit for *all* applications. As we outlined in Chapter 4, "Making the Business Case for Clouds," you have to do the business case around cloud computing to justify cloud computing as the right fit.

However, you will see many startup companies build a significant portion of their IT architecture on cloud computing platforms, since it is so easy to justify the use of cloud computing assets when considering the cost benefit for a startup enterprise. Some startups will place their entire IT infrastructure on the platform of the clouds, from e-mail to calendaring to databases to enterprise applications. They will realize huge cost savings by taking this route and will therefore have a large competitive advantage over their competition.

Considering the advantage that startups will have and that many of those startups will grow to be large enterprises, it is logical to assume that many larger companies in the future that leverage cloud computing from the beginning will continue to be dependent on cloud computing as they become larger, publicly traded companies. That is just a matter of the evolution of this technology and the benefits of adoption as a systemic component of the enterprise architecture or SOA.

Q: Will cost savings continue to be a significant driver for cloud computing?

A: Yes, but it is not the only driver. As we saw in Chapter 4, there can be substantial cost benefits when leveraging cloud computing, but as we pointed out, your mileage may vary. You have to consider the cost holistically with other factors, including strategic benefits that are typically harder to define but there nonetheless.

It is easy to determine that cloud computing is less expensive than traditional on-premise computing by simply considering the operating expenses. The real benefit of cloud computing (or more specifically, SOA using cloud computing) is the less-than-obvious value it brings to an enterprise, including

- The benefit of scaling
- The benefit of agility

The benefit of scaling means that cloud computing provides computing resources on demand. As you need those resources, you simply contact your cloud computing provider and add more capacity by paying more money. You can do this in a very short period of time, typically less than a day, and thus avoid the latency, expense, and risk of going out to purchase hardware and software that takes up data center space and the traditional time required to scale up an application in support of the business.

The use of cloud computing resources allows you to go in the other direction as well. You can remove capacity, and thus expense, as needed to support the business. If the business contracts and the number of transactions are not what they used to be, you can reduce your costs by simply reducing the computing resources within the cloud computing providers. No need to turn off expensive servers and have them idle.

The benefit of agility means that our SOA using cloud computing architecture can be easily changed to accommodate the needs of the business because it uses services that are configured via a configuration or process layer. For instance, if you add a new product line that needs specific processes altered to accommodate the manufacturing, sale, and transportation of that product, those processes are typically changeable by making a configuration change, not by driving redevelopment from the back-end systems.

While this is a core benefit of SOA, in general, the use of cloud computing resources enhances agility, since cloud resources are commissioned and decommissioned as needed to support the architecture and changes to the architecture. You can bind in logistics processes from an application-as-a-service provider that supports the movement of the new product from the factory to the customer. Since you leverage a prebuilt service, out of the clouds, you do not have to suffer through the expense and cost of building that service from scratch.

Moreover, cloud computing does not provide a cost benefit in all cases. You have to closely look at each problem domain and business and do an objective cost analysis to determine the true benefit. The tendency is to go with what seems trendy in the world of enterprise computing. While cloud computing may be of huge benefit to your enterprise IT, you have to consider all of the angles we laid out in Chapter 4.

Q: What about cloud computing standards going forward?

A: Standards are important to SOA and thus should extend to cloud computing. There are over 150 separate SOA standards, called the WS-* standards, ranging from standard ways of doing messaging to standard ways of doing governance. Many in the world of cloud computing consider cloud computing as a new space that needs new standards. The fact is, most of the standards we have worked on in the world of SOA over the past several years are applicable to the world of cloud computing. Cloud computing is simply a change in platform, and the existing architectural standards we leverage should transfer nicely to the cloud computing space.

Having said that, since many consider the cloud computing space to be "new," we will surely see cloud computing–specific standards emerge, perhaps standards that address the need for portability of code and standards interfaces. Those are fine, but we should look at the existing SOA standards in the world of cloud computing, and not create new standards for the sake of creating new standards.

Standards are a double-edged sword; they clearly provide some value by protecting you from vendor-specific standards, in this case, cloud lock-in. However, they can delay things as enterprise ITs wait for the standards to emerge. Moreover, they may not live up to expectations when they do arrive and not provide the anticipated value.

Standards should be driven by existing technologies rather than by defining new standards approaches for new technologies. While the latter does occasionally work, more often it leads to design-by-committee and poor technology. Past failures around standards should make this less of an issue in the world of cloud computing.

So, when considering SOA and cloud computing standards, take a few things into consideration:

- Standards should be driven by three or more technology vendors that actually plan to employ the standard. Watch out for standards that include just one vendor and many consulting organizations.
- Standards should be well defined. This means the devil is in the details, and a true standard should be defined in detail all the way down to the

code level. Conceptual standards that are nothing but white papers are worthless.

- Standards should be in wide use. This means that many projects leverage this standard and the technology that uses the standard, and they are successful with both. In many instances, standards are still concepts and not yet leveraged by technology consumers.
- Standards should be driven by the end users, not by the vendors. At least, that's the way it should be in a perfect world. While the vendors may have had a hand in creating the standards, the consumers of the technology should be the ones driving the definition and direction. Standards that are defined and maintained by vendors often fail to capture the hearts and minds, while standards maintained by technology consumers typically provide more value for the end user and thus live a longer life.

The key advice here is to not let standards drive your architecture. Leverage them where they are needed to support the architecture. The architecture should be fairly stable, while the technology and the enabling standards will surely change over time.

Q: How will SOA and cloud computing exist together in the future?

A: Let's get back to the basics. SOA is an architectural pattern that actually predates the SOA buzzword. It is about breaking architecture down to a functional primitive, understanding the information and behaviors, and building it up again using service interfaces that are abstracted into a configuration layer to create and, more importantly, re-create business solutions. SOA, as the *A* implies, is architecture.

Cloud computing is a platform option, or a way of creating a system in which some or all of its IT resources exist within some third-party cloud computing resource, such as Amazon EC2 (an infrastructure-as-a-service) or Force.com (a platform-as-a-service). Cloud computing is something that can involve part or all of an architecture.

Cloud computing is an architectural option, but it is not architecture unto itself. This will not change as we move forward. SOA should become even more important to this emerging space because it provides guidance as to how the architectures are formed and which target platforms are the correct fit, on-premise and cloud computing–based.

Putting this more simply, SOA is all about the process of defining an IT solution or architecture, while cloud computing is an architectural alternative. Thus, SOA cannot be replaced by cloud computing. In fact, most cloud computing solutions will be defined through SOA. They do not compete: They are complementary notions, as hopefully this book presented to you. Cloud computing and SOA will remain different and complementary concepts.

The role of SOA in cloud computing is systemic. The ability to create a successful cloud computing solution means having an information-, service-, and process-level understanding of the problem domain, as defined in this book. Then, break the architecture down into services that are decomposed and normalized, and define core business processes that leverage those services. Finally, you can pick the technology solution, and cloud computing is another weapon in your architectural arsenal to create a successful instance of an SOA.

Another thing to keep your eye on here is that SOA, while being an architectural pattern, is also a strategy. You need to keep your enterprise architecture and the use of SOA in clear view as you look at any new technology or approach coming down the pike. Again, the technology will always change, whereas your architecture should remain relatively stable.

Never Separate Cloud Computing from SOA

There have been some disturbing tendencies to separate SOA and cloud computing. Many companies feel it is necessary to separate architecture teams for the push into cloud computing, and those new teams are not working with the existing SOA teams. The rationale is that they consider cloud computing to be new and believe it therefore needs a new team with its own budget and different leadership.

Those of you who think you can separate architecture and cloud computing are gravely mistaken. For most of today's projects, the best way to drive toward cloud computing is to leverage SOA approaches, as we describe in this book. This means understanding your problem domain at the data, services, and process levels before moving data, services, and processes out to cloud computing platforms.

continued

The end-state architecture will be a mix of on-premise and cloud computing platforms, and thus the architecture will span on-premise and cloud computing systems. It is architecture, not cloud computing, that will save the day here.

This kind of stuff will continue to pop up until those in IT step back from the hype that surrounds cloud computing. Give them a copy of this book; it is a great place to regain perspective on the core issues. Cloud computing is a great way to go if there is an architectural fit. However, like any technological approach, you have to consider it as an architectural option, not the architecture.

The trouble comes when the cloud computing team lives up to its name-sake and focuses only on creating new processes and moving existing processes to cloud computing. This solves nothing unless there is complete synergy with the existing enterprise systems. In too many cases, synergy seems to be an afterthought.

Q: What about interoperability between cloud computing providers?

A: Extending our discussion of standards, the larger issue concerns interoperability among cloud providers. This is the notion of (1) cloud providers offering built-in communications as well as application and data portability among the cloud computing providers, meaning providers can talk to one another; and (2) cloud providers having the ability to move services, processes, and data among themselves as needed.

Focusing on the first concept, there is another concept known as the *Intercloud*. The Intercloud is the notion that allows cloud providers to exchange information and behavior in support of those who use the cloud. Modeling the Internet, they want to connect many different things together and provide a standard mechanism for doing so.

This connectivity is important for a few reasons. First, it puts the responsibility for communication among providers on the providers' shoulders, and not on the users'. Second, it produces a foundation for interoperability that has been pretty ad hoc. Finally, it reduces the price point of cloud computing, and, considering the previous two points, cost is the core selling point of the clouds.

Cloud providers see the value of promoting interoperability. They might find that interoperability gets many enterprises off the fence and moving toward the clouds. However, the success of interoperability within the cloud providers' realm will depend on their ability to stop building features and start building for interoperability. At the end of the day, cloud users will have to insist on interoperability, as they did in the world of SOA and other architectural shifts in thinking.

Q: What kind of technology skills are required if you want to extend your IT to the clouds?

A: At the core of cloud computing, nothing really changes. You still do storage, database, application development, and application deployment. Now you just do some of these things out of the cloud, as a service. The fundamental computing models we have lived with for many years do not go away.

However, in support of cloud computing, the skills required will be around architecture and platform.

For *architecture skills*, we will need people who understand the business issues and can translate those business issues into requirements and then into architecture. This book is about providing you with that core knowledge so you can be that architect, with a clear understanding of how your existing enterprise IT assets, when driven by the requirements of the business, can translate into a target architecture that may or may not leverage cloud computing.

Platform skills are centered on understanding the target cloud computing platform in detail and how to build or transfer processes, data, and services onto specific cloud offerings. There will be a need for those who understand the larger cloud computing players, such as Amazon and Salesforce.com. However, if you understand the basics of computing resources, such as storage, databases, and application process, then understanding how they are deployed in the cloud is not that much of a leap. You must look specifically at how the cloud computing providers address those concepts, including interfaces, and at development and operations mechanisms that are usually proprietary to the cloud computing provider.

When Clouds Are Built on Clouds

Why build your own cloud computing infrastructure when you can leverage existing cloud computing providers? This is with a trend that many new cloud computing startups are following: building their clouds on existing clouds, such as Amazon and others.

continued

The reason enterprises employ cloud computing platforms is the same reason the startups deploy cloud computing platforms: to access very sophisticated application development and hosting resources without having to invest in hardware, software, and data center spaces. Once upon a time, startups had to obtain a large amount of capital just to get their solutions up and running. Today the platform investment is in as-a-service products, and companies pay only for the resources they leverage.

Cloud computing startups can now use their investment to build their own intellectual capital or their own cloud computing solutions using the existing cloud providers' platforms to accomplish their goals. This is a beautiful model, considering the cost advantages. And the hard architectural issues around multitenancy, security, and even governance are solved for them at the platform level. This means startups can focus on what is unique and different about their solution.

This trend will continue as more and more cloud computing startups launch and the existing cloud computing platforms provide the core services that those startups need to build, deploy, and operate their own cloud computing solutions. Gone are the days when you had to have your own hardware and software to be a cloud computing or traditional software company. Today, it is all available to you on-demand.

Cloud computing removes the barriers for many startups to get their solutions out there, and the number of cloud computing providers offering solutions of interest to the enterprise is increasing—exploding—because the barriers to entry are nonexistent.

Q: What about performance and cloud computing?

A: There are two issues around performance as related to cloud computing: network latency and platform performance.

The fundamental model of cloud computing is dependent on the Internet, so any reliability issues or performance issues with the Internet will affect the cloud computing solution. Organizations often do not consider network latency issues in conjunction with cloud computing, but the issues can and do exist, including network saturation at critical times when the cloud-delivered resource becomes the slow link in the long architectural chain. In other words, the on-premise systems respond as per expectations, but cloud computing-based systems respond too slowly due to network latency issues.

Performance related to *network latency* typically arises around large data sets being sent to and from the cloud computing provider. The larger the data set, the more likely network performance issues will come into play. You can take steps to mediate the issues around network performance by understanding the network performance issues that may arise through performance modeling and testing and by designing the applications, services, data, and processes to minimize the use of the network. Since you have to pay for bandwidth, you save money as well as make your overall architecture perform better.

Network performance modeling is the concept of creating models that determine how the network will perform under an increasing load and using that model to determine saturation points. It is a good idea to perform this step, at least at a rudimentary level, to understand any network performance issues that will affect your cloud computing solution before they happen. However, given the "bursty" nature of the Internet and the wide variations in network performance from time to time, this is not an exact science.

As an option, some cloud computing providers allow you to leverage dedicated connections into the data centers that host the cloud computing platform, providing a dedicated pipe between your enterprise and the cloud computing provider. This, of course, tremendously decreases the chances that you will have performance issues. However, it also increases the cost.

Platform performance centers on the performance of the cloud computing platform itself. Most cloud computing platforms leverage a shared, multi-tenant, virtual architecture. You have your own virtual space, or virtual machine, but you share processors and storage space with hundreds, perhaps thousands, of other users on that cloud platform. It is conceivable that the cloud computing platform will become saturated from time to time, and thus performance issues could arise.

There is not much you can do about this, other than work with your cloud computing provider to insure that you get the performance you require. Many enterprises insist on service-level agreements, or SLAs. These are legal agreements that require the cloud computing platform to provide a specific level of performance.

Other things you can do to protect yourself include extensive testing of the cloud computing provider at different times of the day before you accept the platform. Or, you can simply call existing customers of that cloud computing provider and ask them specifically about performance. There are no guarantees here, and one of the downsides of leveraging a cloud computing platform is that you do not own or control those systems.

Q: What about security and cloud computing?

A: Many who push back on cloud computing point to the security risks as a reason not to leverage cloud computing platforms. The reality is that cloud computing does not mean you give up security. You can support an exceptional level of security and leverage a cloud computing platform. It is just a matter of establishing the right security model, selecting the right security approaches and technology, and working with the cloud computing provider to make sure they adhere to those models, approaches, and technology.

Most cloud computing providers are very aware that security has to exist and work for them to be successful. They have thought through many different security models and patterns to provide to their users, including encryption, role-based security, identity management, and more. The trick is to think through your security requirements before you select a cloud computing provider, and make sure they support your requirements.

Q: What is the future of cloud computing and SOA using cloud computing?

A: In a word, bright. We could consider cloud computing as a revolution in the way we do computing going forward and something that will overshadow architectural patterns such as SOA. However, cloud computing will be more of an evolution than a revolution. As time goes on, we will find more of our core enterprise services, processes, and data on cloud computing platforms.

This will be a slow migration. While many are calling for the "big switch," it will initially be a "switch in bits." Traditional enterprises will move to cloud computing platforms as it makes sense for them, and only a few systems at a time. Considering the importance of core business systems, this is only prudent.

Just a few years ago, traditional enterprise IT would not have thought any major enterprise systems would run outside of their control. The advent of software-as-a-service and/or application-as-a-service, including Salesforce.com, taught us that existing enterprise IT will not implode when they leverage enterprise applications that exist outside of the firewall and thus outside of their control. The core benefits, including speed to deployment and cost, are too great to ignore.

As we move more infrastructure-type resources to cloud computing platforms, including storage, databases, transaction processing, and application development, this requires more of a shift in thinking than when we leveraged only software-as-a-service or applications-as-a-service. SOA using cloud computing means we are willing to leverage more fine-grained IT resources that are delivered as a service, and to mix and match those resources in the context of our architecture to support the business.

Going forward, the adoption of these fine-grained resources will define how our architecture, specifically SOA, extends into cloud computing. We could have our databases hosted with one provider, our application development platform with another, and our process server and rules engine with a third. In other words, we can spread the architecture to the cloud computing providers that provide the best functionality and reliability at the best price, and we can have cloud computing–delivered resources work seamlessly with all on-premise resources.

Cloud computing is nothing to be afraid of. It is a fundamental evolution of the way we do computing. At the very least, it will provide a well-defined architectural option for those who build enterprise architectures using SOA approaches. The core idea of cloud computing is to open up your mind and your architecture to any sort of technology that will allow you to better serve the business.

Index

Addison-Wesley Information Technology Series

Cloud Computing and SOA Convergence in Your Enterprise

A Step-by-Step Guide

David S. Linthicum

FREE Online Edition

Your purchase of *Cloud Computing and SOA Convergence in Your Enterprise* includes access to a free online edition for 45 days through the Safari Books Online subscription service. Nearly every Addison-Wesley Professional book is available online through Safari Books Online, along with more than 5,000 other technical books and videos from publishers such as Cisco Press, Exam Cram, IBM Press, O'Reilly, Prentice Hall, Que, and Sams.

SAFARI BOOKS ONLINE allows you to search for a specific answer, cut and paste code, download chapters, and stay current with emerging technologies.

Activate your FREE Online Edition at
www.informit.com/safarifree

> **STEP 1:** Enter the coupon code: DAAGTZG.

> **STEP 2:** New Safari users, complete the brief registration form.
> Safari subscribers, just log in.

If you have difficulty registering on Safari or accessing the online edition,
please e-mail customer-service@safaribooksonline.com

Adobe Press   ALPHA   Cisco Press   FT Press   IBM Press   lynda.com   Microsoft Press   New Riders

O'REILLY   Peachpit Press   PRENTICE HALL   QUE   Redbooks   SAMS   SAS Publishing   Sun microsystems   WILEY